Why Do I Have to Read This?

Literacy Strategies to Engage Our Most Reluctant Students

CRIS **TOVANI**

Stenhouse
PUBLISHERS

PORTSMOUTH, NEW HAMPSHIRE

Stenhouse Publishers
www.stenhouse.com

Library of Congress Cataloging-in-Publication Data
Names: Tovani, Cris, author.
Title: Why do I have to read this? : literacy strategies to engage our most
  reluctant students / Cris Tovani.
Description: Portsmouth, New Hampshire : Stenhouse Publishers, [2020] |
  Includes bibliographical references and index. |
Identifiers: LCCN 2020019100 (print) | LCCN 2020019101 (ebook) | ISBN
  9781625311511 (paperback) | ISBN 9781625311528 (ebook)
Subjects: LCSH: Reading--Remedial teaching.
Classification: LCC LB1050.5 .T665 2020 (print) | LCC LB1050.5 (ebook) |
  DDC 372.43--dc23
LC record available at https://lccn.loc.gov/2020019100
LC ebook record available at https://lccn.loc.gov/2020019101

Cover illustration and design by Ari Eppert. Interior design and typesetting by Cindy Butler.

Manufactured in the United States of America

PRINTED ON 30% PCW
  RECYCLED PAPER

26 25 24 23 22 21   9 8 7 6 5 4 3 2

For Sam, who is sometimes my brain—ok—a lot of times my brain.

Contents

Acknowledgments

Teaching is incredibly complex, so educators need ongoing ways to investigate how students learn best. Years ago, Sam Bennett and I started a project that provided opportunities for teachers to study student engagement. These first Literacy Labs began over twenty years ago, observing my students in action. Like scientists in a laboratory, we wanted ways to explore the good, the bad, and the ugly of classroom instruction. We knew that if teachers had opportunities to collaborate, research, and study my students, instructional shifts would happen. When teachers asked to study their own kids, we began setting up Lit Labs in different districts all over the country.

Reading and writing well is incredibly complex, and students are asked to do it every day. Working on this book has been a constant reminder of just how cognitively challenging reading and writing are—especially when one doesn't feel like doing them. Many of the stories in this book come from students who attended Evergreen Public Schools in Vancouver, Washington. I am thankful for the countless kids like Caleb, Vanessa, Devon, Olivia, Natalie, and Mallorie, who let me be their temporary teacher while others watched their every move.

Collaborating with colleagues is incredibly complex, and sharing your students with a stranger is scary. I am thankful for teachers like Anna Capacci and Steve Massart who served as the teachers of record for the classes I taught. They helped me navigate copy machines, technology glitches, and district policies. Special thanks to Mandy Ollila, who also served as a teacher of record. She wasn't so hot with the technology, but she was amazing when it came to following up with kids and tracking down permission slips.

Being an instructional leader is incredibly complex, but Karrie Fansler makes it look easy. Karrie is a learning design specialist in Evergreen Public Schools, where I was able to teach for two years. Karrie made sure that in between my visits, teachers received feedback and coaching. She organized labs, worked with instructional coaches, and brought administrators into the fold of Literacy Lab learning. A position like Karrie's is made possible when district leaders are visionaries and know that when teachers' learning is taken care of, students benefit most. I am thankful for the following bigwigs: Bill Oman, Michael

Espinosa, Judy Wallis, Colleen O'Brien, Alisa Wills-Keely, Stephanie Jerauld, Rachel Thompson, Rochelle Daniels, Tammy Hays, Libby James, David Herrera, and Scott Wolf for supporting and sustaining Literacy Labs in their districts.

Being a building administrator is incredibly complex because there are countless plates that require constant spinning. I am grateful for the administrators who supported the idea of letting their teachers study and develop a workshop model that worked for their students. Thanks to Danny Orrantia, Lynnette Sundstrom, Julie Tumelty, Allison Harding, Charles Anthony, and Andrea Wooster, who invited me into their buildings to work with teachers and students. This group brilliantly designed a plan that melded credit recovery classes with professional development. While I worked with students in the mornings, teachers studied student engagement. In the afternoons, they collaborated to design compelling units. They read research and figured out how to make instructional shifts that aligned best practices to their teaching beliefs.

Publishing a book is incredibly complex and doesn't happen because one person decides she has a good idea. I am thankful for the folks at Stenhouse who patiently awaited this fourth book. Thanks to Bill Varner for his gentle nudging. Thanks also to Amanda Bondi, Cindy Butler, and Shannon St. Peter for their copyedits and production design. Posthumous thanks to Chandra Lowe, who was always ready with a word of encouragement and an answer to a question whenever I needed it. I miss you, Chandra.

Editing your friend's writing is incredibly complex, especially when she doesn't like to be told what to do. However, without Sam Bennett, this book would not have been possible. Sam is not only my instructional coach and part-time editor, but she is also my best pal who did whatever it took to keep me writing. She kept meticulous observation notes that captured students' conversations so that I could recreate real-time teaching and learning. Sam's clear thinking enabled me to turn a mess of ideas into a hopefully, useful book. (She also planned very cool writing breaks that gave me energy to dig back into writing.)

Let's face it, right now, everything seems complex. We need each other when it comes to teaching the next generation to read and write well. I am thankful for the educators on the front lines. They are brave and hardworking and they do what it takes to serve students. It is teachers who give me hope that we will survive these challenging times.

Chapter 1

I Hate School and
I'm Not Wild About You Either

Six days of double blocked classes and all I've gotten out of Ugo is dirty looks. When I try to confer with him, he puts his head on his desk. When I ask him what he needs to get started, he shrugs his shoulders. When I tell him to "get busy," he shoots me a glare.

At lunch, I pull Ugo's folder out of the period one basket to see if he has any written work that will give me a clue about him as a learner. He seems angry. He won't talk with me. To be honest, I'm a bit intimidated by this 6-foot junior, who gives me sidelong glances when I ask him what he thinks. Before going to my office, I head down to the lunchroom to get a cup of coffee. I think about Ugo as I walk toward the noise of the cafeteria.

I turn the corner and enter the student commons, and there I see him. Ugo is laughing and messing around with a bunch of his buddies. Unfortunately, I have to walk right past his group to get my coffee. If Ugo doesn't want to talk to me in class, he sure isn't going to talk to me in front of his friends. I decide to pretend that I don't see him. As I get closer, I spot him listening to a friend and then see a huge smile spread across his face. He grins from ear to ear, and I am struck by his bright, white, perfectly straight teeth. *Hmmm*, I think, *maybe this kid isn't so scary, after all*. Maybe I just annoy him. Maybe he just hates his English class.

I look past Ugo and his group. I pick up the pace of my walk. As I pass, Ugo stops laughing, looks my way and says, "Hey, Ms. Tovani," and then turns back to his friends.

Surprised, I stammer, "Hi Ugo." I get my coffee and as I head back to my office, I think, *I've got to see that smile again*. On Wednesday, Ugo will be my first conference. I'm going to see what's behind his mask of defiance.

We've all had students who appear angry and defiant and maybe for good reason. Ugo did his best those first six days of class to keep me away from him. But when I saw Ugo with his friends, he wasn't wearing his anger mask. I would later learn that his tough-guy bravado was a way to keep teachers from knowing how afraid he was of failing again.

These Kids Don't Care

When students don't do what we want them to, it's frustrating. At workshops, I am frequently asked these questions:

- "How do I get students to think for themselves?"

- "How do I get kids to care about the learning?"

- "What do I do with kids who won't read and write?"

- "What do I do when kids don't care enough about their work to revise?"

- "What do I do if they can't read grade-level material?"

- "What do I do with students who don't care or aren't motivated to do anything?"

Teaching is complex. My whole career, I've tried to figure out answers to these questions. It seems like every week there are new layers to uncover. Lately, I've been studying how students "show up" to class each day. Depending on the day, the same kid can walk into class with a different attitude for learning. It's almost as if he is wearing a mask to help him get through the period. On the days when students struggle to engage, they seem to be wearing a mask that puts a barrier between themselves and me. Depending on the mask they are wearing, my response changes. If a student is angry, I respond very differently than if he is clowning around. How I respond can either cement the mask on the kid's face for the day, or it can remove it so the student is ready to learn. The first step is recognizing the mask.

The Masks Kids Wear

I cringe a little when I hear a teacher refer to a group of students as "my low-level learners" or say, "So-and-so has always been a C student." Here's why: no one performs at the same level all the time. In physical education, I mostly wore the mask of confidence. Growing up with three brothers forced me to compete with males who were older and stronger than I was. When it came time to compete with my own gender and age, I had an advantage over other girls in my class. However, I struggled in algebra, and so I donned the mask of a class clown to avoid embarrassment when I didn't get answers fast enough. In language arts, I wore the mask of minimal effort, and was known to comment on how stupid everything was. I did this to cover up my struggle to comprehend.

No one wakes up in the morning, looks in the mirror, and says, "Boy, I hope I do terrible today." When I encounter tough students who I struggle to engage, I try to remember the different masks I wore. Recognizing students' masks and remembering that each one serves a purpose helps me to honor and discover what they need. Sometimes the mask helps a kid save face or fit in. Other times, it helps them avoid something they struggle with or keeps the teacher from getting too close. Masks are not only a way for students to protect themselves, but also to try out who they want to become.

Sometimes those masks give us the impression that kids don't care or that they are unreachable. In many cases, the mask is armor that protects them from the stinging bite of failure. When I think about students in this way, it gives me empathy and energizes me so I don't give up on the ones who appear unteachable.

You've just met Ugo, who wore the mask of anger and apathy during the first six days of school. For stories of other students like him, check out Chapter 3.

The Mask of the Class Clown

Julian wore his class clown mask on the days he came in late. He'd make a grand entrance doing something ridiculous so that everyone knew he was there. On those days, he loved pulling kids away from their work. If he could make someone laugh, it meant they were off task too and he'd have a partner in crime. When Julian felt most vulnerable, he wore the mask of the class clown.

Everyone loves a comedian, but only for so long. The antics of the class clown get old rather quickly. When students wear this mask, they mimic the teacher and ask silly questions. They yell out comments and look around the room hoping to get a rise out of other students. Teachers can find themselves spending more time trying to get this student on task than teaching the other thirty-two kids in the room. It sometimes feels that the only way any teaching and learning can happen is if the student and his class clown mask are sent to the dean.

Over the years, I've had a lot of kids who wore the mask of the class clown. I suspect that it was a way to avoid what they hated doing—reading and writing. The class clown mask provides an excellent shield that enables students to avoid what they don't like to do. They wear this mask to distract the teacher from making them do the hard work of learning. Their attempt to entertain is just a way to hide their lack of confidence and skill level for what teachers are asking them to do.

If you've ever had any kids like Julian, you will relate to the stories in Chapter 4. Along with the anecdotes are strategies to help you meet the needs of students who wear this mask, so they and everyone else in class can get down to business.

The Mask of Minimal Effort

Kids who wear the mask of minimal effort can often be heard saying things like this:

"This is boring."

"I'm done."

"I'm way ahead of my group so if I participate, I'll spoil it for everyone."

"This is so easy."

"This is good enough."

"I did this last year."

"I don't care; I just need the points."

Kellen wore the mask of minimal effort. The first day of class she made sure that I knew she was already an excellent reader and writer as evidenced by the many AP classes she had taken. When she wasn't telling someone how to do something, she was rolling her eyes and acting aloof.

When I asked her why she was in my English class instead of AP Literature, she said, "I need an easy A, so I decided to take your class instead. Plus, I heard it's fun."

I was pleased word had gotten around that my class was fun, but I was also a little irritated that she thought she already had an easy A.

During the second week of class, students turned in their first draft of a commentary comparing conditions from an excerpt of George Orwell's *1984* to ours in the present. Kellen's first and what she thought final draft was about the integration of church and state, a piece I suspected she had written for another class. Initially, Kellen faked me out. Did I miss something in the *1984* excerpt that Kellen noticed? Was it me, or did several of her sentences seem out of place, as if they had been cut and pasted from another source? Could the draft she turned in for me be an assignment for another class? Maybe AP Government?

Kellen was the fixed mindset poster child. The daughter of a teacher, she had always been told she was an excellent student. For her, the thought of not getting the A or failing in front of her peers was frightening. At the beginning of the semester, she put on the mask of minimal effort to project competence and hide the reality that she didn't do everything perfectly the first time. When I provided feedback and time to revise, she started to feel more comfortable admitting that she needed more than one attempt to produce something of high quality. Soon she expected and accepted opportunities to revise, and the mask of minimal effort came out less often.

Mauricio, on the other hand, learned that doing the bare minimum helped him fly under the radar. He adeptly wore this mask when asked to do something he saw no purpose for. He told me on the first day of class that he was only coming to school so that he could graduate. Period. Being undocumented meant his chances of going onto college were slim. He was fluent in Spanish and English and knew that a high school diploma would enable him to get a better-paying job as a crew chief with a local roofer. He didn't want to argue, and he certainly didn't want to waste any brain power reading novels or doing a writing assignment that only his teacher would read. "Just tell me what I need to do to pass," he'd say. "I don't really care about English. I just need the credit so I can graduate."

For three weeks, Mauricio put in his seat time in return for his passing grade. When he turned in his writing, he asked, "This is good enough, right?"

"For a first draft, it is."

"I don't really redo work," he said.

"OK," I said. "But I hope you aren't embarrassed when the businessperson you send it to reads it."

"Businessperson?" he queried.

"Yeah, we're sending the final copies to local businesses so they can hear what their future workers think."

"But, I don't write very good."

"That's why you're in school," I smile. "Everyone needs more than one chance to write something well. How do you want to make your letter better?"

Mauricio picked up his learning target rubric and pointed to the last target. He read, "*I can call my readers to action*. What does this mean," he asked?

I handed him my open letter and said, "OK, read the last paragraph, where I wrote my call to action. See what you notice. When you are finished, let me know, and I'll help you start yours." He took my example and headed back to his seat.

In the end, Mauricio chose to send his writing to a local construction company, explaining the importance of business owners helping undocumented workers get their green cards and work permits. When he got a response from the owner, something changed for him. I can't help but think that having a real audience and purpose forced him to take off the mask of minimal effort. He still had a lot of writing lessons to learn. But when he heard back from the construction company I think he learned a more important lesson: his voice mattered. When Mauricio recognized a greater purpose than just playing the game of school, he wore his mask less often.

If Kellen and Mauricio sound like students you've had before, and you'd like to hear stories of how we worked together to remove the mask of minimal effort, Chapter 5 is where you might start.

The Mask of Invisibility

"Take the next few minutes," I announce, "to wrap up your reading and writing. Be thoughtful about what you bring to your group. Collect any new aha moments or questions you want to share." With about twenty minutes of class left, it's time for students to reflect on and debrief today's learning with their discussion groups.

I watch as students prepare to talk. Some kids shuffle through annotated articles and prioritize what they want to share first. Others have their thinking held on sticky notes, and a few have thinksheets with quotes from their readings that they want to talk about.

As I scan the room, Grace catches my eye. She dutifully organizes her folder. I wonder if she will talk in her group today to share what she has figured out. Today is the first time I've conferred with Grace. She is compliant, quiet, and never seems to need me. But during our conference, her thinking surprises me. Initially, she is hesitant to talk. Grace doesn't respond to my open-ended questions. If getting her to talk is all I rely on to know what she understands, I will be stuck. I ask to see her folder where her thinking is held. Looking at her thinksheets, I invite her to pull out the one that she thinks is important. She immediately goes to a double-entry diary and points to the third entry. I read what she wrote and a big smile crosses my face. *This kid is deep*, I think to myself. How have I missed her?

Grace has figured out something that I never thought of. I hope that she will share some thinking with her group. To increase the chances, I announce to the class, "If you're lucky enough to be in Grace's group, be sure you invite her to share. What she figured out today is amazing." I look over at Grace. She continues to organize her folder and doesn't look up, but from where I'm standing, I think I can see the corner of her mouth cracking a slight smile.

Kids who wear the mask of invisibility can be easy to forget. They don't make waves. They don't blurt out every thought that comes to mind. Sometimes they excel and other times they barely squeak by. The worse thing about accepting that kids who wear the mask of invisibility are just shy is that we miss the opportunity to see so much good thinking. If you have any students like Grace, and you'd like to know more about the kids who slip through the cracks, you might begin with Chapter 6.

Whether you teach language arts or math, science or social studies, you know these kids. We all have them. They are the ones who keep us up at night. This book isn't just for English teachers; it's for all teachers who have kids who struggle to read, write, and participate in class. Hopefully the ideas in this book will spark new ways for you to address the behaviors of your most disengaged learners. As you read the examples, think about how you could tweak them to work for you and your students. I've included strategies that can be easily adapted to all content areas. As you read this book, I hope that you'll be energized with new ways to engage students so that you can spend more time teaching and less time coaxing kids to behave.

When Am I Fully Engaged?

High engagement leads to high achievement. Low engagement leads to low achievement.

—John Guthrie

Flash back to three years ago. My twenty-five-year-old calls and asks if I'd like to go to hot yoga with her later in the week. In my head I am thinking, *Nooo.* Hot yoga is the last place that I want to go, but to spend time with my daughter, I'd go just about anywhere. So, I lie and say, "Sure, I'd love to."

Friday rolls around, and as I pull into the parking lot I see a space next to my daughter, Caroline, who is already there. As I get out of the car, she gives me a funny look, "Is that what you are wearing?" In an attempt to cover up my out-of-shape body, I'm wearing heavy gym shorts that go to my knees and a giant T-shirt that hits me at the elbows.

"Yeah, what's wrong with it?" Never having been to a yoga class before, I'm not really sure what to wear, but I know I probably won't be going again, so why spend money on an outfit? My daughter nods her head and says, "You're going to be hot." She then asks if I have a yoga mat.

"Nope," I say. "But no worries. I'm sure I can rent one inside."

Caroline shrugs her shoulders and says, "OK."

We walk into the studio and I get another funny look from the twenty-year-old working behind the counter, who of course is in perfect shape. I infer her look is because my outfit is all wrong and I'm so out of shape. After taking my money for the class and the mat, Miss Perfect Body says, "Um, you might want a towel," and she hands me a 4-by-6-inch piece of terry cloth. With a vocal fry she says, "Put this on your mat; it might help you."

At this point, I feel like a giant practical joke is being played on me. I thought I knew what yoga was. I thought that I would get some good stretching in, listen to some zither music while deep breathing, and maybe chant a few mantras. Boy, was I wrong. Within five minutes I'm sweating profusely. My feet slip, and I feel like I might as well be surfing as doing a sun salutation. Out of embarrassment, I laugh to cover up my mistakes, only to notice that everyone in the class is completely serious. No one talks to me or even smiles to make me feel better. It isn't long before I notice that people have slid their mats as far away from me as they can. I get more sidelong glances and I know that I am out of my element.

The class finally ends, and it seems like my daughter is ignoring me. *She must just be tired*, I think. Heading to our cars, I get the same feeling I did twelve years ago when I dropped her off at the mall as a middle schooler. It dawns on me that I've embarrassed her.

Now, this story makes my daughter sound like a brat. She really isn't. She thought I had done yoga before. After all, I do acupuncture and take Chinese herbs. I sometimes read books about Eastern religions. How could I have NOT done yoga? I felt bad that I had embarrassed her, but the competitive side of me said, *You need to redeem yourself.* So, I started taking semiprivate yoga lessons. I learned how to modify positions so I didn't hurt myself. I purchased the proper attire so that I didn't pass out from dehydration. I got my own mat with only my sweat on it. And even though I'm not great at yoga, I can now go to class with my daughter and not be an embarrassment. Three years later, I continue to do yoga on my own. I now recognize the importance of the practice and its payoffs. But what did it take for me to fully engage?

Circles of Engagement: Behavioral, Emotional, and Cognitive

When I think about the different types of connections to engagement, I realize that initially, the only reason I went to yoga was to connect and engage with my daughter. That's what hooked me. The emotional connection alone, however, wasn't enough. So, I started to learn the behaviors of yogis. I learned what to wear, how to adapt the poses, what equipment to bring, and how to behave. I no longer laugh and cause a ruckus in class. When I started to experience the health benefits of the practice—improved balance, flexibility, and state of mind—I started to appreciate the need to "know" yoga. For me, initial engagement happened because I wanted to spend time with my adult daughter. It wasn't because I wanted to learn yoga.

While working on the book *No More Telling as Teaching: Less Lecture, More Engaged Learning* (Moje and Tovani 2017), I came across a body of research that investigated student engagement at school. Researchers Jennifer Fredricks, Phyllis Blumenfeld, and Alison Paris identify that when students are engaged behaviorally, emotionally, and cognitively, teachers can almost guarantee that they are learning.

However, hitting the sweet spot where kids are engaged at all three levels is hard to do without planning.

Planning for engagement means thinking about how to hook kids in the head, heart, and gut every day. I think about the following questions when planning for that sweet spot:

> **Behavioral:** What behaviors, skills, strategies, and mindsets do students need in order to engage in the work? What strategies do they need to read and write complex text? What classroom systems and structures need to be in place so that students can work without relying on me running the show?

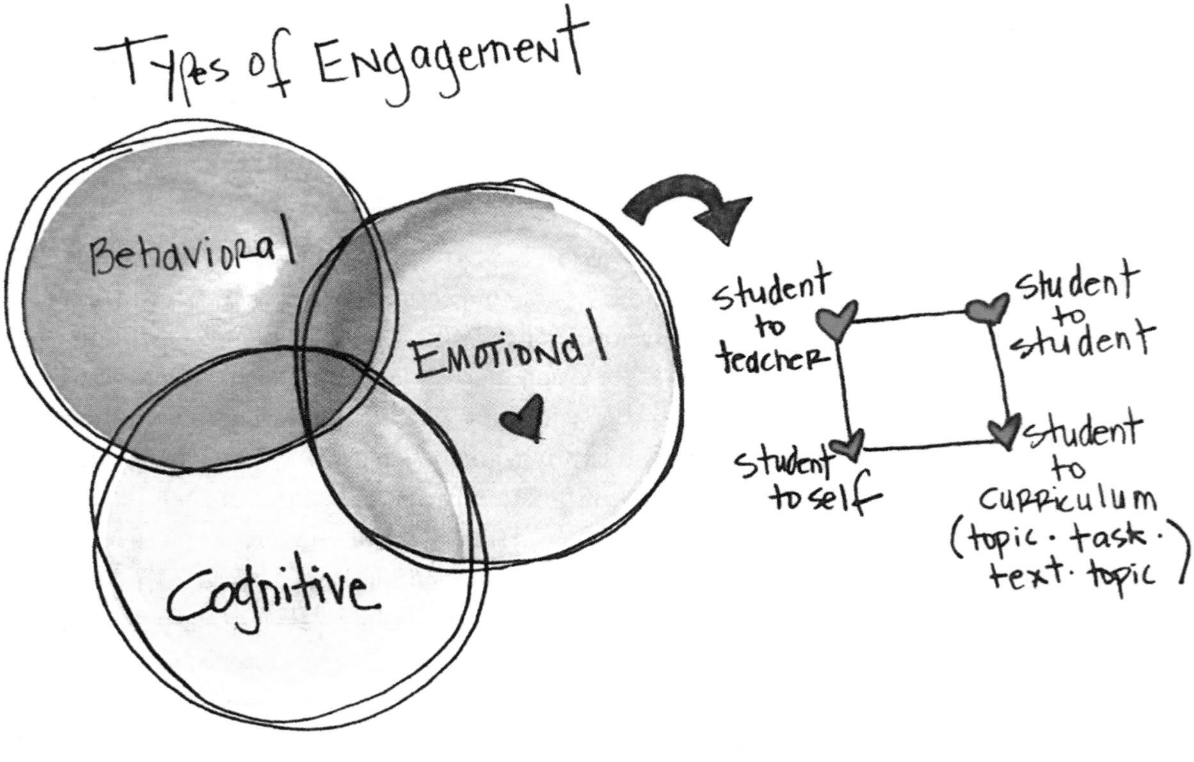

Types of Engagement

Behavioral

Emotional

Cognitive

student to teacher

student to student

student to self

student to curriculum (topic · task · text · topic)

Credit: Samantha Bennett

Figure 1.1
Circles of Engagement

Emotional: Why should students care about the topic, their classmates, and their own learning? What makes the topic compelling? What images, quotes, and real-life stories can the teacher share to hook them in the heart and make them care about the unit of study? What do I know about students that lets me connect to them? How do I set up systems and structures that encourage students to connect and collaborate with each other?

Cognitive: Is the work that I'm asking students to do worthy of their time? Why does knowing about the topic matter? How will knowing this information empower students outside of the classroom? What will students remember about their learning ten years from now? What is the purpose of the work they are doing now?

What Comes First?

Recently, a middle school teacher asked, "Do kids have to be behaviorally engaged before they can get emotionally and cognitively engaged?" It was an interesting question and one that I hadn't thought of before. Conventional wisdom says that in order for kids to learn, they have to behave or understand the behaviors of a discipline. Others might argue that there must be a purpose for the learning if students are going to engage. For some, engagement starts with making a connection to a topic, a need, a goal, or a person.

Thinking back to the teacher's question, "What kind of engagement comes first?" I don't think there is one right way to engage learners. But if I plan with the idea of making connections to their head, heart, and gut, I have more options to hook more kids for more minutes each class period. If John Guthrie's research is right, and high engagement leads to high achievement, then more minutes of engagement means more minutes of learning (Guthrie 2004).

Back to Our Big Questions

Earlier in this chapter, I shared the questions I get asked the most. This time, I'd like to add a layer that will outline the rest of this book to help us think about how we can work smarter to influence our most reluctant and recalcitrant learners.

- **How do I get students** who wear the masks of disengagement **to think for themselves?**

- **How do I get kids** who wear the masks of disengagement **to care about their learning?**

- **What do I do with kids** who wear the masks of disengagement **to get them to read and write?**

- **What do I do when kids** who wear the masks of disengagement **don't care enough about their work to revise?**

- **What do I do if kids** who wear the masks of disengagement **can't read grade-level material?**

- **What do I do with students** who wear the masks of disengagement **who don't care or aren't motivated to do anything?**

Throughout the book, I share stories of kids that you will recognize. In these stories, you'll read about big fails and also some successes in my efforts to meet the needs of students who wear the masks of disengagement.

In Chapter 2, we'll tackle how to use our time to best influence student learning. When students come to us with too many needs, and wear the mask of "I'm not doing it," what CAN we actually do? How do we refuse to play the shame-and-blame game and overcome feelings of despair? How we spend our time, in and out of the classroom, can make a big impact on how we meet students' needs. I'll introduce the idea of **CYA: C**urriculum **Y**ou **A**nticipate— **structures** that will help you plan long-term units and teach you how to nest goals each day so that daily work in the classroom feels connected. Not only will content and skills stick with students longer, but they will also see how to better access and wield power in the world.

In Chapter 3, we'll explore how CYA structures can support students who show up wearing the masks of anger, apathy, or both. We'll dig into strategies that will disarm and redirect these learners so they can engage and learn.

In Chapter 4, we'll laugh with and at the antics of our class clowns. We'll think about how to ensure each day is worthy of their time, so the jokers become more sophisticated in their humor and less like the kid who makes obscene noises in the back of the classroom. Chapter 4 is filled with many concrete CYA structures for you to try.

In Chapter 5, we'll hear stories about both the overconfident and the compliant—two sides of the same "I'm done" coin. How do we ensure students can re-engage in tasks that are worth their time? And how do we name what matters and why it matters by using products that professionals in the world create as our mentor texts. Again, I'll name the concrete daily and long-term CYA structures that will help you reach these learners.

In Chapter 6, we'll notice the kids who put on the mask of invisibility, and we'll discuss what they need to be part of the learning community. I've included an array of thinksheets that will give kids who wear the mask of invisibility a way to show you what they know.

I'll wrap things up in Chapter 7, and you'll be patting yourself on the back as you appreciate your power as a teacher who plans. Knowing that you have new ways to engage kids will give you energy to get back into the classroom and teach!

Remember, this book isn't just for ELA teachers. But, if your students are all succeeding, then this book is not for you. If no one in your room ever puts their head on their desk or repeatedly asks to go to the bathroom, then you don't need this book. If you've got it all figured out, then for goodness' sake, go buy yourself a treat with the money you would have spent. You've earned it.

But, if you've ever had a student who you just couldn't hook, or a group of kids who you were sure were conspiring against you, then this book could come in handy. If you find yourself more exhausted than your students, then the **C**urriculum **Y**ou **A**nticipate structures, introduced in Chapter 2 and illuminated in Chapters 3–6, might give you some new ways to re-engage those hard-to-engage kids. Yes, you will be CYA-ing yourself by using these structures to plan. If you are just a little stuck, maybe the stories of my students will remind you that you aren't alone and help you find an entry point for yours.

I argue that teaching is more complex than directing a play. Teachers can't expect the same plot and set of characters every day like directors can. Based on students' needs, the masks they choose to wear can change from class to class and day to day. Sometimes, they'll put on the anger mask. Other days, they might don the mask of the class clown or the perpetually bored student. When teachers are able to recognize the masks that students wear and trust that each one serves a purpose, they can target students' needs. Teachers' efforts to better plan and use instructional strategies to re-engage students isn't a waste of time. Knowing that we can make a difference in the lives of kids every day is when our teacher superpowers are strongest!

After three decades of teaching, I'm still trying to figure out how to reach kids who are frustrated or act like they don't care. I want to help those who struggle to read and write at every grade level be successful. If students understand that being able to read and write better will not only make life easier but more enriching, we will all have a better standard of living. If you are a teacher who wants to serve all kids, even the ones who play hard to get, this book is for you.

Chapter 2

Wedgies, Drunken Bears, and the Stress of Shortsighted Planning

I could have saved myself a lot of grief and stress had I planned for more than a week at a time.

—Tamara, high school teacher in Charleston, South Carolina

Halfway through my teaching career, I received my first unsolicited coaching letter. It rocked my world and forever changed who I was as a teacher.

Let me back up a bit. My second book, *Do I Really Have to Teach Reading?* (Tovani 2003), had been out for about a year, and as a result teachers from all over North America wanted to visit my classroom. I was teaching full-time and felt like I was drowning trying to meet the needs of my own students and of the teachers who wanted to see everything I'd written about. To alleviate some stress I asked my colleague Sam Bennett, who had brought local teachers to my classroom earlier in the year, to facilitate visitors from South Dakota. With Sam facilitating, I could focus on my students and their learning.

I'm embarrassed to admit that I was exhausted, and as a result, planning for some of my classes took a back seat. To say I was burning the candle at both ends was an understatement.

At the time, I taught on a 95-minute A/B block schedule, which meant I only had two classes on the day of the South Dakota teacher visit. One was senior-level English, and the other was reading intervention.

I wasn't worried about the visitors seeing my first hour. That was a breeze. 9/11 was still fresh in everyone's mind, and students were engrossed in Khaled Hosseini's novel *The Kite Runner*. I chose that book as the anchor text because of its compelling story. I also knew that I could find lots of powerful nonfiction for kids to read that would help them understand our increasingly complex world.

Unfortunately for the students, visitors, and me, I did not have a long-term unit planned for second hour. The reading intervention class was designed as a good old-fashioned Reader's Workshop. I relied heavily on the three main components of workshop model: minilesson, work time, and debrief. Ideally, my day-to-day "plan" was to let students read their self-selected books after I did a minilesson on a literacy strategy. When kids were released to read, I would confer or work with small groups. During the debrief, students would write in their response journals and then share out their thinking with their tablemates.

However, the plan didn't match reality. Getting thirty striving, aliterate, and uninterested readers to simply read for joy while I conferred was a joke. Every day, work time felt like a game of whack-a-mole. I'd get one side of the room reading, but meanwhile, the other side exploded in chaos. Without real reasons to read and write, most students wouldn't engage.

Like all veteran teachers, I knew how to do the dog and pony show, so I thought I knew how to plan for the visitors to avoid disaster. In my mind, all I had to do was find some high-interest short text, model a thinking strategy, throw in a few fillers, and plan a few "catches."

On a Sunday morning I sat down with the newspaper and began to look for something that the kids would read. A few pages in, I found it. Right before the entertainment section, at the end of the local news, were four short news items. The first piece was about a dancing bear that performed much better when drunk. A local animal rights organization was suing the entertainment group for animal cruelty. I would use this story to model my questions and then think aloud, showing how my background knowledge could help me infer. Students would then practice using these strategies on the second piece, which was about the dangers of wedgies and the damage they can cause when done without restraint. Drunken bears, animal cruelty, and wedgies—what ninth grader wouldn't care about these topics?

That Monday morning, Sam showed up early with bagels for the prebrief. We welcomed our visitors, discussed our observation norms, and modeled how to take notes for the debrief. The kids arrived and we were off to the races—me teaching two back-to-back 95-minute lessons with twenty adults observing my every move.

Needless to say, second hour was a disaster. But had the visitors noticed? I saw them taking notes, but what did they write? If they had noticed, maybe they would take it easy on me since they also taught struggling readers. In a few short minutes, we'd start the debrief and I would know. I trusted Sam to facilitate the conversation, and I knew she would keep me safe. She'd guide the visitors as they fleshed out what they saw and heard, and she'd help them label why it mattered to learning.

The debrief went fine, thanks to Sam focusing visitors on what they saw first hour and spinning what they saw in second hour. They were full from what they'd observed and learned, and eager to get back to their classrooms to try new ideas. We said our goodbyes, and I let out a sigh of relief. I planned to quickly apologize to Sam for the second-hour disaster and then put this day behind me. Before I could even get out "Sorry about second period," Sam hit me with a brutal observation: "Today was hard for me as a facilitator. I felt like I saw two different teachers. You trusted seniors to dive into an important topic, and you gave freshmen an article about drunken bears. I almost feel like what I saw was a violation of students' civil rights. It doesn't seem like the same respect was there for kids in second period as there was in first."

"Whoa! Respect? Civil rights?" I snapped. "Are you kidding me? What happened today had nothing to do with respect or violating students' civil rights. It had to do with surviving another day with struggling readers. Do you know how hard I've tried to hook these kids?" I asked. "You know that they all hate to read. Right?" Silence filled the room. In my head, I answered the question for her: *No, you don't know. And because you don't walk in my shoes, you don't know what they need.*

In my mind's eye, I can still see Sam packing up her computer as I huff into my office. Wisely, we kept our mouths shut and politely said goodbye. But I was angry. I felt as if an outsider had sashayed into my room and told me how to teach. I knew that second period was a bust and that students needed something more. I just didn't know what it was.

Trust Them to Think

A week went by, and even though I hadn't seen Sam, I was still thinking about second hour. Was I being disrespectful to students by having a laser focus on strategy instruction versus studying a compelling topic? Did I believe in them? Did I trust them to read, write, and discuss a gripping topic? That afternoon, in my inbox was an email from Sam. *Surely*, I thought, *it must be an apology for the way she acted*. It wasn't.

Here's the letter that rocked me:

> *Dear Cris,*
>
> *Thank you for including me in your recent series of labs with both local and national visitors and for digging into the hard work of getting smarter together. It has been really great to spend so much time together. You make me think hard and examine what I believe matters most to create powerful, literate citizens who will soon join our ranks in the world. I'm thankful that they have you as a role model of an engaged, enthusiastic participant of life.*

Pondering this paragraph, I can't tell if Sam means what she writes or if she's throwing shade. First hour is definitely getting smarter about the world, but based on what she saw during second hour, she can't possibly think I'm doing a good job preparing students to "join our ranks in the world." My goal was just to get them to read better.

Following her initial paragraph, I see that Sam has described and tracked how minutes were used during first period. I see that I talked for twenty-two minutes and kids worked for the other seventy-three. She labeled the clear purpose for the lesson and used direct quotes from students to support how they built background knowledge and grew their skills.

Then, she moved on to second hour:

> *I noticed you framed period two around strategy instruction: questioning and accessing background knowledge to infer. Here is the breakdown of activities and how each chunk of time was used for you to present/model (T) and for students to read, write, and talk (S).*

Then she gave me the brutal breakdown of how minutes were used during second period:

T=Teacher talk time; S=Student work time

1. *9:27 a.m.–9:37 a.m. Introduction of visitors and talk about Mt. Rushmore*

   Remember, the visitors were from South Dakota, and because I hadn't planned for the long-term, I needed filler.

Use of Minutes:	
Teacher	Students
10	0

2. *9:37 a.m.–10:02 a.m. Show a political cartoon, let students talk about it in small groups, groups share out*

   Political cartoons can be powerful short texts that allow kids to practice inferring. Unfortunately, the cartoon I chose didn't connect to anything I had planned that day.

Use of Minutes:	
Teacher	Students
17	8

3. *10:02 a.m.–10:11 a.m. Cris introduces the minilesson: "When someone says, 'Draw a conclusion or infer the answer,' what does he or she mean?" Students write in their notebooks what they think it means and then turn to a partner to discuss.*

Use of Minutes:	
Teacher	Students
6	3

4. *10:11 a.m.–10:15 a.m. Conversation Calendars—Cris responds to a student's question about how to use them.*

Use of Minutes:	
Teacher	Students
4	0

5. *Article focus:*

10:15 a.m.–10:26 a.m. Cris models thinking with the drunken bear article

10:26 a.m.–10:37 a.m. Students hold their thinking on the wedgie article

10:37 a.m.–10:42 a.m. Talk as group about the wedgie article

10:42 a.m.–10:47 a.m. Try to answer one question you wrote on the article with a possible, probable answer

Use of Minutes:	
Teacher	Students
11	
	11
	5
	5

Not included in the breakdown is a description of the chaos. Me running from kid to kid to get them on task because they didn't want to read so they weren't asking questions or inferring answers.

6. *10:47 a.m.–10:57 a.m. Students stood against the wall—Cris asked, "Where are you on the spectrum of getting it to not getting it?"*

Use of Minutes:	
Teacher	Students
9	1

To be honest, I have no idea what I was trying to do here. I think I was going for some activity that would get kids moving in hopes they would settle down to read. It was stupid.

7. *10:57 a.m.–11:02 a.m. Visitors shared with the students what they noticed about their learning.*

Use of Minutes:	
Teacher	Students
5	0

These teachers were very polite Midwesterners, which meant they had to lie to honor the kids and what they saw.

Reading how the minutes were used is stunning—but not in a good way. For sixty-two minutes, I talked and tried to corral kids, meaning only thirty-three minutes were left for them to work. Two-thirds *me*, one-third *them*—the REVERSE of first period.

I immediately start rehashing what I should have done. I guess I should have started with better text. Maybe some juicy questions would have kept kids from getting bored. But how would I do that with strategy instruction?

Sam ended her letter with some questions of her own and a challenge for me:

- *How would you describe students' purpose today in class ONE? Whose thinking surprised you? Who frustrated you? What's next as you think about growth for each student?*

- *How would you describe students' purpose today in class TWO? Whose thinking surprised you? Who frustrated you? What's next as you think about growth for each student?*

- *From the time-breakdown above, what strikes you about:*

  - *Time for learning?*

  - *Connections tied to purpose for learning?*

  - *How do you plan? What are you wondering about planning?*

I'm really intrigued to hear what you think about each of your two classes today. I know we don't have a formal "coaching" relationship, but I'm sure teachers are going to want to continue to see your brilliance in action, and I'd love to know more about your process so I can be of better use to them and to you.

Please write back to me SOON before the tides of life sweep you away. Just type for five minutes and press send. Hearing your thinking will help me be a better facilitator, and it might give you more energy too, as you continue to grow students and teachers from all over the country into incredible citizens. We need MORE of them to be as actively engaged as YOU are as a human and professional. Thanks.

Love,
Sam

Our Big Questions

In the book *Make It Stick: The Science of Successful Learning*, authors Peter Brown, Henry Roediger, and Mark McDaniel argue that the way we teach in many schools defies current cognitive science (2014). Conventional wisdom tells us that before we can move on to a more complex concept or skill, we have to master the basics. Students are frequently directed to learn one concept or skill before moving onto another (mass practice). However, current cognitive science suggests that when learners have a chance to spiral back to recurring ideas with more complexity, (interleaved practice) they build context and add layers of meaning to their learning. In the spirit of cognitive science, and interleaving, let's revisit our provocative questions for the book:

- **How do I get students** who wear the masks of disengagement **to think for themselves?**

- **How do I get kids** who wear the masks of disengagement **to care about their learning?**

- **What do I do with kids** who wear the masks of disengagement **to get them to read and write?**

- **What do I do when kids** who wear the masks of disengagement **don't care enough about their work to revise?**

- **What do I do if kids** who wear the masks of disengagement **can't read grade-level material?**

- **What do I do with students** who wear the masks of disengagement **who don't care or aren't motivated to do anything?**

Each question from the list above is connected in some way to lack of engagement—sometimes behavioral, sometimes emotional, sometimes cognitive. When I try to control another person, I get exhausted. However, focusing on what I can influence leaves me with more energy to teach.

When I get stuck trying to figure out how to get kids to do something, I create a two-column table. On the left-hand side, I write down all the possible reasons why students aren't doing what I want them to do. On the right-hand side, I brainstorm strategies that I can put into place to address what students need and influence how they learn.

When I ask teachers to brainstorm all the possible reasons students might disengage, a pattern starts to emerge:

Students Disengage Because They Have . . .
Parents divorcing
Cell phones
Hunger
Boredom
A tough homelife
Reading issues and inability to access the text they've been assigned
Mental/physical health issues
Tasks assigned that are too hard or easy
No pencil or other materials
Fear of taking a risk
No idea where to start
No idea what the criteria of success look like
No purpose for the learning

What would you add to this list of items that pull your kids from learning?

As teachers, we are notorious for burning ourselves out, focusing on issues we have little or no control over. Sometimes those issues even become excuses we make for students not to engage. For example, "My students have a horrible homelife, so I just need to love them." Of course we need to love our students. But that's not enough. We must also engage them so they are empowered with abilities to access information and communicate thinking. Fixing a students' homelife is out of our control. Focusing on issues that we have little ability to influence zaps our energy and leaves us with less time to work on what we can change or improve.

To help teachers focus on what they can influence, I ask them to review their list of items that cause students to disengage and cross off any that they can't do anything about. For example, *parents are divorcing*. Unless the teacher is the one causing the divorce, they have no control over that problem. I instruct teachers to cross that one off the list. Another issue that teachers worry about is student hunger.

Food insecurity is a serious issue that communities and districts need to better address. Teachers alone can't solve this problem. They can attempt to address it by keeping a stash of breakfast bars in their coat closet, but that gets expensive. They can also contact the building social worker and connect the student with a local food bank or a social service agency that might help. But for the most part, teachers can't solve the issue by feeding every hungry student they have.

Students Disengage Because They Have . . .
~~Parents divorcing~~
Cell phones
~~Hunger~~
Boredom
~~A tough homelife~~
Reading issues and inability to access the text they've been assigned
Mental/physical health issues
Tasks assigned that are too hard or easy
No pencil or other materials
Fear of taking a risk
No idea where to start
No idea what the criteria of success look like
No purpose for the learning

Once we cross off what we can't fix, we can begin planning for the items that we can influence. Teachers often mention that their students complain of boredom. When I ask teachers if they can influence students' boredom, their knee-jerk response is no. When I pause and give them a second to think about it, many nod their heads and say maybe.

We have a lot of sway over student boredom. We're the ones planning the lessons. We have dedicated our lives to teaching our content, and we are the ones who get paid to teach it. So, if students are bored, it might be time for us to revisit or rediscover why the topics we teach are amazing, important, and useful.

When I think about my own learning and what compels me to learn, certain conditions come to mind:

- I am curious about the topic. I have questions that I want to find answers to.

- There is a purpose to the learning. I can see how it will help me to do something in my day-to-day life.

- I can collaborate with someone and share with others what I've learned.

- I have a model of what success looks like.

- I have the right materials and equipment to engage.

- I have fun while engaging in the learning.

- There is gratification attached to the new learning.

What makes learning compelling for you?

When I revisit this, I consider the implications of how I spend my time both **inside and outside** of class. Am I using it in a way that optimizes and influences student engagement?

Ways to Influence Students' Learning Inside and Outside of Class

Students disengage because they have...	What can I influence *in class* when students are with me?	What can I influence *outside of class* when I'm planning with student engagement in mind?
~~Parents divorcing~~ Cell phones ~~Hunger~~ Boredom ~~A tough homelife~~ Reading issues and inability to access the text they've been assigned Mental/physical health issues Tasks assigned that are too hard or easy No pencil or other materials Fear of taking a risk No idea where to start No idea what the criteria of success look like No purpose for the learning	I can spend time talking to students one-on-one and in small groups to learn more about what makes *each* student tick. I can make connections to my own experiences, to other students, to content, to the world outside of school, and to other texts so students know they are not alone. I can model ways for them to tackle the task or text. I can model different ways to negotiate struggle. I can set a purpose and provide a clear vision for the lesson. I can share reasons why learning the topic matters. I can coach students as they work to hit the learning targets. I can provide a variety of ways for students to demonstrate what they know and need. I can design a variety of smaller tasks that help students produce a complex final product with an authentic purpose and audience.	Find a compelling topic to cradle the standards. Ask questions that will provoke students to read, write, and discuss. Collect a variety of text structures, genres, and reading levels so students can build background knowledge. Identify learning targets connected to the standards. Identify what students will make to demonstrate that they've hit the targets. Find models of authentic products to show students what "quality" work looks like.

Table 2.1

If we want to hook more students behaviorally, emotionally, and cognitively, we have to figure out how to harness the time we spend outside of class in order to influence student engagement *during* class. Letting go of what we can't influence and anticipating what students might need keeps us and students from burning out.

Planning Ahead to Keep from Getting Behind

I still feel the sting of Sam's observation. I never did respond to her email and it wasn't until years later that I even acknowledged getting it. Her coaching letter held the mirror up to my poorly planned face and forced me to see some truths. Here's what I can articulate now . . .

Planning for my second-semester seniors was interesting and fun, because the testing pressure was off. In six months, the majority of these seniors would be moving on—some heading to college, some considering enlisting in the armed forces, and all eligible to vote in the next general election. Using their last precious months of high school to examine literary elements or memorize SAT vocabulary lists just didn't seem worthy of their time. I had to go bigger.

At the time, grown-ups and teenagers alike were trying to make sense of the events of September 11, 2001. People were wrestling with the idea that a terrorist group, not a country, had attacked the United States. In order to make sense of the anchor text *Kite Runner*, in the context of our current times, we'd dig into the history of Afghanistan and build our background knowledge about its cultures and traditions. We'd also have to figure out who this "Taliban" group was and why most of the highjacked planes were piloted by people of Saudi decent and not people of Afghan decent. We'd have to learn more about bin Laden and try to understand why the US was carpet bombing Afghanistan when he was Saudi. Who was this guy and why did he hate America so much? There were so many authentic questions that would provoke students to read, write, and discuss.

I had identified learning targets with this class, and I knew how students could demonstrate that they had hit them. At the end of the unit, students would write commentaries to the *Denver Post* (CO) to educate and inspire others with their thoughts about current events. They would have a clear understanding that this was not a war against another country; it was a war against ideas, which made the nature of the conflict very different from any that had come before it. I wanted students to build awareness of the multidimensionality of the Muslim faith and cultures in order to cull their fears of the "other." Students would continue to improve their craft of writing argument. They'd investigate the politics and controversies surrounding the war in Afghanistan. Because the unit was relevant, and connected to current events, text fell into my lap. I wasn't scrambling every morning to find something for students to read. Germane text was everywhere, and students had a lot of choices to build their background knowledge about this compelling topic.

Thanks to my long-term planning efforts, first hour hummed with purposeful reading and writing. My daily planning was seamless—I had rituals and routines in place, and not only did I know where we were headed with the study, the students did too.

Prior to the week that the South Dakota visitors joined us, I found a disturbing article about the rise of self-immolation among Afghan women since the Taliban takeover. The article was photocopied and ready to go. Students would read it and annotate questions so I could see what they needed next. It would also give them information that they could tap into as they wrote commentary to submit to the local paper. My minilesson was connected to that task.

I was confident that visitors would see lots of student engagement during first hour. My long-term planning enabled me to differentiate for students. They had numerous reading choices and ways to revise their writing. Productive small-group discussions among students happened several times during the period. The 95-minute class flew by. Unfortunately, what visitors saw second hour was an entirely different scenario.

Winging Workshop

When people asked how I planned for reading intervention classes, my mantra was, "I just find great text." Well, with this class "finding great text" wasn't enough. Looking back, great text alone isn't enough for any class. Most adolescents who struggle and avoid reading aren't spontaneously going to read because an adult has found some "awesome," random piece of text.

Unlike first hour, second hour had no compelling topic to cradle the reading and writing. There were no provocative questions for students to study. I hadn't written clear learning targets for kids to shoot for or designed any "big makes" for them to show their progress. Each day lived in isolation, connected only by the thinking strategies and the components of workshop model. Every day felt like starting over again.

It was no wonder that when the South Dakota visitors joined us in October, I still hadn't jelled with this group of kids. I kept asking myself, *How do I get these kids to read and write?* Students weren't responding to the strategies I was modeling, and why should they? Many had been in a reading intervention class since second grade. The last thing they cared about was visitors coming to see firsthand what I talked about in my books. On that particular Monday, with that particular class, it became glaringly obvious that strategy instruction and "great" text weren't enough.

When Sam challenged me to compare the opportunities I was providing for each of my classes and to consider how I might plan so that all students could go deeper, she somehow changed the way I thought about equity and access. I pledged to never again ask students to read disconnected texts just for the sake of practicing comprehension strategies.

Thinking About the Long and Short of It: Long-Term Planning That Guides the Day-to-Day Work

Teaching thinking strategies in isolation isn't enough to engage any student, let alone striving, reluctant, and aliterate students. Knowing how to use thinking strategies matters, a lot. But there has to be something more, something bigger for kids to sink their teeth into as they journey to become lifelong readers, writers, and thinkers.

I wince reflecting back on the day kids read about drunken bears and wedgies. But I don't know a teacher whose exhaustion, at some point in their career, hasn't led to a haphazardly planned class period on occasion. To be honest, I don't know how I sustained workshop model as long as I did without long-term planning. In retrospect, I was always scrambling to find the next text and strategy that I'd share with kids. More and more mornings I found myself getting to school earlier and earlier to beat the mysterious morning bandit who would jam the copy machine and then bail. Instead of getting ready for kids, I was on my hands and knees prying copy paper from greasy wheels and gears. Wasting my time doing this only increased my stress level because I knew that if I didn't get my copies made, I couldn't keep kids busy.

Every day I provided opportunities for students to read, write, and discuss, but often those days lived in isolation. When students didn't feel like reading the text I provided, or discussing their thinking around the strategy I modeled, I exhausted myself trying to keep them on task.

Moving from one day to the next without a long-term plan put a ton of pressure on me to be an entertainer and taskmaster. I was good at building relationships with students, and that went a long way toward getting them to do what I wanted. Sure, there were always a few kids who didn't like me and some with whom I struggled to connect. Sadly, my heavy reliance on emotional engagement lead me to give up on them too soon. To assuage the guilt, I assured myself that the universe would put someone else in the path of these students who could reach them—justifying that there were lots of learners I had reached that other teachers had given up on.

"It's a waste of time," I would cry when someone asked me to do long-term planning. How could I do that for students I didn't know? I worried that not knowing who my students were would lead me to plan something that was too hard or not interesting. Sometimes I would even brag that I was way more creative when I wasn't tied to a unit. Baloney! All I did was add more stress to my day.

There are two problems with this "fly by the seat of your pants" style of teaching. First, when we aren't clear about what we want students to know and be able to do at the end, it's easy to get off track. Before I created long-term plans, I often found myself bird walking during class or stressing out before class, waiting at the copy machine because I had found something "cool" for kids to read. Second, I would get exhausted trying to get everyone to hit a standard when the standard hadn't even been identified. Without a long-term plan, it's too easy to lose the laser focus on where we are going and why.

When there is a long-term plan in place, the day-to-day teaching is less stressful. Creating a unit in which no day lives in isolation is challenging, but when I do it, it frees me up to do more differentiation during the day when I'm with students.

When I set out to do long-term planning, I consider the following questions:

- What standards do I want students to hit?

- How will students show me they've hit the standards? What might they make and/or do at the end of the unit (e.g., big makes or summative assessments)?

- How will I provide daily opportunities for students to show me their thinking as they work towards more complex tasks/makes (e.g., little makes or formative assessments)?

- Why is the topic worthy of students' time? How will it help them access or use power in their world?

- What questions might provoke students to read, write, and talk?

- What kinds of resources should I start collecting so students can build their background knowledge and practice reading with a variety of text structures?

- What learning targets do I need to identify that will support daily learning? What minilessons can I plan to scaffold the diverse needs of students?

Imagine how much stress we could alleviate if we addressed a few of these questions before we met our students. Long-term planning doesn't mean detailing out every class period for the next eight weeks. It means that we identify a direction to get to a destination. Long-term planning is the road map that keeps me on track. When I know my final destination, bumps in the road don't throw me off. I can take a quick detour and get right back on track. When I don't have a long-term plan, I can almost guarantee that kids don't reach the destination on time.

Curriculum Is More Than the "Stuff" We Teach

Every teacher has been told during their undergrad work or during a mandatory professional development day that they should differentiate for students' needs. That's all fine and well, but how does one do that for 125–180 students? I've learned over the years that if I can't manage something, I stop doing it. Anyone who has been in the classroom for more than fifteen minutes, knows that no single thing works for all learners. When I think about the different masks that kids come to class wearing, I recognize that I must anticipate a lot of needs if I'm going to have any degree of success differentiating. The time to do this work happens before I even meet my students.

Before differentiation can start, prep work has to be done. I picture a doctor preparing for surgery, trying to anticipate possible surprises. After scrubbing, they inventory their tools. They inspect the scalpels, needles, retractors, and clamps. Lasers to cut and cauterize are at the ready. For tight places, the doctor inspects the camera at the end of the endoscopic slicer, making sure it works properly so that there is a clear view when the instrument snakes through the body. When convinced all the monitors are working and the protocols are in place, the surgeon is ready to operate. They have tried to account for and anticipate what the patient might need. This prep work frees the doctor to make real-time adjustments during the operation.

Teachers who work to manage and differentiate instruction are akin to doctors who work to meet the needs of their patients. Doctors only work with one patient at a time. Teachers don't have that luxury. They are expected to work with numerous students at any given moment. If we are to meet a variety of needs for a variety of students, we too have to do prep work. Like doctors, teachers arm themselves with tools, knowledge, and strategies to do their job.

We also have something called "curriculum." When I started teaching, I thought curriculum was the notebook I was handed by the department chair at the beginning of the year. As I gained experience, I equated curriculum with the "stuff" I created with other teachers over the summer. I got paid to fill big notebooks with ideas and scope and sequences but never found them very useful. Over the years, those curriculum guides sat on the top shelf in my office and gathered dust. Only when I was given a new guide did I take the old, dusty one down.

But curriculum is more than our content and the stuff we ask kids to do. It wasn't until I read Steven Wolk's book *Being Good: Rethinking Classroom Management and Student Discipline* that I realized curriculum was a lot more than worksheets, tests, films, and novels. Wolk's quotation of Kathleen B. deMarrias and Margaret B. LeCompte's (1999) definition helped me expand how I thought of curriculum:

> More than the formal content of lessons taught—which is what most people normally think of when they envision curriculum—it is also the method of presentation, the way in which students are grouped in classes, the manner in which time and tasks are organized, and the interaction within classrooms. The term curriculum refers to the total school experience provided to students, whether planned or unplanned by educators. (233)

Wolk adds to the defintion, ". . . curriculum includes everything teachers do . . ." (Wolk 2002). This means that if I truly want to attempt differentiation, I need to have some planning structures in place that will engage students not only for the class period, but for the entire unit.

CYA Structures: Harnessing the Power of the Six Ts: Topic, Tasks, Targets, Text, Tend to Me, and Time

After a day of professional learning, an instructional coach asked if she could talk to me before I left for the airport. She said, "You've given teachers and me so many things to think about. I'm worried that it's just too much. If I were going to model some small bites of what you do to get kids engaged, what would they be?"

In a hurry to catch a plane, I couldn't give her a very good answer. But her question intrigued me. So, I started keeping a list of actions and structures that I put into place to engage and re-engage students. Curious to know if there was a pattern, I started labeling them with a planning structure that was part of the design principles of the EngageNY literacy curriculum (now called Education Language Arts Curriculum) and described in the professional book *Transformational Literacy* (Berger, Woodfin, Plaut, and Dobbertin 2014, 92). To encourage engagement, the developers of the curriculum advocate planning units with Four Ts in mind: Topic, Task, Targets, and Text. I categorized many of my actions and structures using the Four Ts. However, there were several items for which this structure didn't fit. I noticed many times I wasn't really teaching but tending to a student's needs. Sometimes I was providing a pencil or just asking them how they were doing. I also saw that I didn't live by the pacing guide. If a student needed more time to complete a task, I let them do it. If a group of students or an individual was ready to move on, I adjusted the daily work time to fit their needs.

I keep Maslow's hierarchy of needs in the back of my mind. I remind myself that I can't feed, clothe, and ensure that all students have shelter and sleep. But I can help students feel safe and included. I can also scaffold their learning for their success which fuels their self-esteem. I recognized that I made allowances for personal needs and time, noting that not all students run by the same clock and learn at the same speed. In order to categorize all my actions and structures, I added two more Ts: **Tend to me** and **Time.**

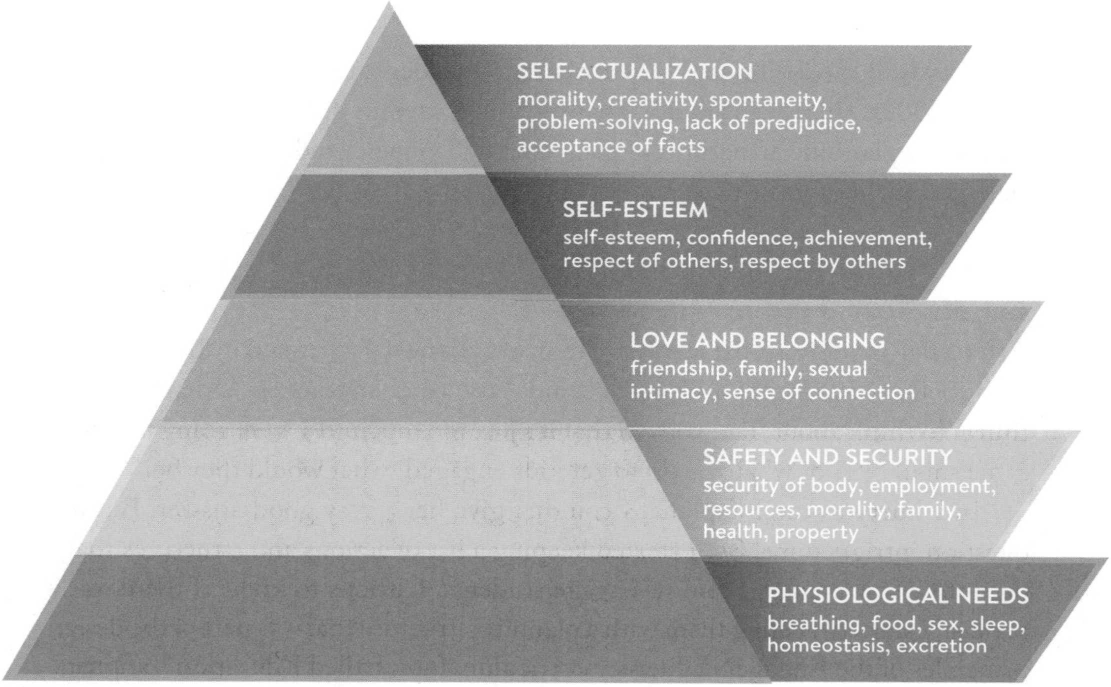

Figure 2.1   Maslow's Hierarchy of Needs

Looking at the list of planning structures, I realized that not only did I use these Six Ts to plan units, but I also used them to tweak plans and re-engage students on a day-to-day basis. While in mixed company, I refer to these concrete ideas, linked to the Six Ts, as **C**urriculum **Y**ou **A**nticipate structures (CYAs). But when I'm working with secondary teachers I refer to them as Cover Your Ass structures. As crass as that label sounds, it's accurate. When we plan for students ahead of time using the Six Ts, like surgeons do with patients they treat, we can better meet students' needs in the moment.

When I use the Six Ts to think about long-term and daily planning, I can make instructional shifts more easily. The Six Ts help me anticipate, manage, and differentiate for a variety of students and situations. You will notice that the structures overlap and not every structure is used in every situation. In each of the following chapters, I show how unit-based planning structures make the daily work easier. Using the questions in the table below, I can anticipate and plan for the pitfalls that often cause students to disengage. (Remember, this isn't just for ELA teachers. I use these questions when I work in other content areas as well.)

CYA Structures: Questions that help me prepare and anticipate curricular needs of students

T	As a Unit-Based Planning Structure	As a Daily Planning Structure
Topic	What topic am I asked to teach? How might I frame it with case studies, provocative questions, and connections to the world outside of school? Why is this topic worthy of students' time? Why do students need to know about this topic? What is essential? What do I want them to remember and be able to do ten years from now? How will understanding the big idea or developing these skills help students be better human beings?	What does this student already know about this topic? What life experiences or interests does this student have that might connect to the topic we are studying? If the student doesn't care about a particular case study (e.g., rollercoasters' connections to force and motion), how might I substitute a different case study or example (e.g., concussions' connections to force and motion) so the student connects to and re-engages with the topic?
Task	What do professionals in the world who understand this topic create? What do they do? What will students do that is authentic, and why is this task worthy of students' time?	How does the task I am asking students to do TODAY (e.g., annotate the text) connect to what I'll ask them to do in the future (e.g., use details from the reading to support an argument)? Do students have a clear understanding why today's task matters to their long-term learning? How will I show the readers/writers/thinkers in the room how I tackle the daily/long-term task as the most experienced learner in the room?
Target	Can I name the MOST IMPORTANT key concepts, knowledge, habits, and skills I want students to develop over the course of this unit? What concept, knowledge, skill, and habit targets are worthy of students' time?	What do students need today to help them reach the long-term targets? (concept, knowledge, habit, skill) What patterns did I see in students' work today that will help me write targets I didn't anticipate in my initial planning? What minilessons do students need to help them work longer?

Table 2.2

T	As a Unit-Based Planning Structure	As a Daily Planning Structure
Text	What variety of resources will I collect and make available for students to build their background knowledge, provoke thinking, analyze content/craft, and practice growing their skills as readers and writers? What variety of resources will I use/create/make available as models of what I'll ask students to create?	What variety of texts do I need today/this week to ensure each reader/writer/thinker grows? How will I connect each student to a "just right" text—in content, form, and topic—to both feed their curiosity and help them grow? How will I show the readers in the room how I make meaning/get unstuck when I read? How will I show the writers in the room how I get started, add thinking, organize my thinking, and revise?
Tend	What do I know and need to know about my students and the local issues in the news/community? How does that knowledge help me narrow the topic to something they and the community might care about?	What am I noticing about the needs of students so I can plan for 1-1 or 1-small-group conferring? Who needs me MOST to get unstuck today? Who do I need to know more about? Who haven't I checked in with for a while? Who am I wondering about?
Time	How much time will learners need to build their background knowledge and develop skills linked to the big ideas? When I did my own assignment, how long did it take me to produce a high-quality piece of work? How much time in class vs. outside of class will I expect learners to dedicate to build background knowledge and to produce high-quality work? How many days will I build in for students to write and create with multiple rounds of revision? How much time do I need to gather an authentic audience with whom students will share their thinking?	How much time will THIS learner, on THIS day need for these task(s)? How much time will THIS learner need to hit the targets? What **combination of minutes** of read, write, talk will work for this student, or for different groups of students on this day? What **sequence** of read, write, talk will work for this student (or smaller groups of students) for this particular day, task, and target?

Table 2.2 (continued)

The Six Ts help me to think about the unit and how I will ensure students work towards the standards on a daily basis. I think about a topic for a unit of study that is compelling enough for students to wrestle with longer than a few class periods. I consider what kids will make at the end of the unit to demonstrate they've hit the standards. I recognize that hitting national standards is a big leap for some learners, so I consider what supporting, nested learning targets students might need to reach the long-term target. I search for an anchor text and shorter companion pieces that will give students context for the topic. I plan on my calendar a six-to-eight-week unit to be sure there is time for students to receive feedback and revise thinking. Last, I consider how I will structure daily work time in a way that will allow me to confer with students, giving attention to their individual learning needs.

I also use the Six Ts on a class-to-class basis to quickly assess why a student is off task and what they might need to get back on track. It's almost like a formative assessment in my head. If a student is disengaged, I consider if they need a different:

- Reason or case study to dig into the topic?

- Task to show thinking and understanding?

- Target to scaffold learning?

- Text to access content and information?

- Way for me to tend to the student's needs?

- Time frame to complete and learn the task?

The Six Ts help me anticipate what students need and give me day-to-day entry points to help with engagement. When students disengage, I don't have to throw out the whole unit or give up on a kid when the solution could be altering one of the Ts. Students can also use the Six Ts to reflect on their own learning and what they might need to do or change to dig back into the work. It gives them agency to be in charge of their own learning.

The Six Ts Organized by Small Bites: Topic, Tasks, Targets, Text, Tend to Me, and Time

Thanks to the instructional coach who asked me what one small bite she and her teachers could try, I jotted down a few actions and structures teachers could try when a student is reluctant or refuses to engage. You will notice overlapping structures because some are so powerful that they address multiple needs. Think about one of your most disengaged students. Which bite would you start with?

Master List of General CYA Structures to Try (long-term and daily planning strategies mixed in!)

Topic-Related	Task-Related	Target-Related
• Know and be able to articulate why a topic or unit of study is compelling. • Find topics worthy of study connected to current events that are conflict-laden, edgy, and compelling. For example, nuclear weapons, gun control, civil rights, and viral outbreak. • Construct questions that provoke students to read, write, and talk; use those questions to drive daily inquiry. • Kick off the unit with a short text to create curiosity. • For classes where the final demonstration of understanding is a test (ACT, SAT, AP, IB exams) use the website's philosophy to show how the work prepares students for high-stakes assessments by connecting the higher-order thinking skills to the daily work.	• Arrange desks into tables instead of rows so students can talk and collaborate, allowing them to build background knowledge, to share ideas, and to feel connected. Consider using chat rooms when students work virtually. • Use thinksheets instead of worksheets so that students have different ways to show their thinking (see Chapter 6 for examples). • If the task is reading-based, model in short spurts how to think about a chunk of the complex text instead of reading it aloud and telling kids what it means. • If the task is writing-based: model how to get started, add thinking, get unstuck, or revise along the way. • Label what students do and patterns you notice in class versus what they don't or can't do.	• Post clearly written learning targets in student-friendly language. • Make time for students to reflect on the targets. Do they understand what they mean and why they matter? • Vary targets so that there is a combination of concepts, knowledge, skills, behaviors, and habits that students shoot for. • Formulate small groups and base instruction on needs. • Provide short, written feedback to the targets on students' work to encourage and push thinking. • Provide minilessons that connect to the targets and are responsive to students' needs. • Plan daily as well as larger assignments to identify key targets and to anticipate and prevent student roadblocks.

Table 2.3

Text-Related	Time-Related	Tend to Me
• Pair nonfiction with fiction text so students have context for the literary work or topic.	• Build in two-thirds of the time in each lesson for students to read, write, and talk.	• Label what students do and patterns you notice in class versus what they don't or can't do.
• Pair fiction with nonfiction text so students care about the factual information.	• When students are set to task, the teacher CONFERS 1-1 or 1-small group to get smarter about what students need.	• Model a variety of ways to show thinking (No fill in the blanks, copy notes from the screen, or only annotate with certain responses).
• Provide unconventional text such as tweets, social media, cartoons, and photos to generate curiosity.	• Confer with at least three-to-five kids per class.	• Provide clean copies of text with wide, blank borders so students have room to annotate thinking.
• Provide choice by selecting a variety of text structures, including different genres and media. Include a variety of reading levels so students can build background knowledge and increase their agency and ownership.	• Provide time for students to build and activate background knowledge and to be able to ask questions without penalty or fear of embarrassment for being wrong.	• Provide an authentic audience for students to share their work.
• Provide a variety of text structures and levels of texts for students to access content and build their comprehension skills by increasing their minutes of practice.	• Give students time to own the targets by allowing them to reflect and understand why the targets matter. Assess if they understand their purpose and how they will spend their time in their quest for learning concepts, knowledge, skills, behaviors, and habits.	• Provide examples (weak and strong models to show criteria of success).
• Provide a variety of text structures and levels of texts so students can build disciplinary vocabulary.	• Build in time for students to revise. What tasks can be taken off of some students' plates so they can spend time on skills that will matter most to their growth?	• Give students time to analyze models for both content and craft.
• Model a variety of ways to show thinking (avoid fill-in-the-blanks or copy notes).		• Formulate small groups and base instruction on students' needs to revise or complete the task.
• Start with short texts to create curiosity.		• Provide short, written feedback on students' work to personalize, encourage, and direct learning.
• Provide digital and clean copies of text with wide, blank borders so students have room to annotate thinking.		• Provide minilessons that are responsive to student work on the task.
		• When planning daily and long-term assignments, make an effort to gauge the time, resources, and skills students will need to keep going.

Table 2.3 (continued)

Tend to Me, Con't

- Group desks into tables instead of rows so students can get to know one another and feel connected. Consider using chat rooms when students work virtually.

- Learn and use students' names quickly; insist that students do the same.

- Get smarter about one kid in every class, every day. Figure out who they are beyond their student identity.

- Confer with at least three-to-five kids per class.

- Formulate small groups, and base targeted modeling and instruction on needs.

- Provide minilessons that are responsive to student needs.

- When doing daily as well as larger assignments ahead of time, consider what students will struggle with and what they might need to keep going.

When conferring 1-1 or with small groups consider the following:

- Model in short spurts how to think about complex text instead of reading it aloud and telling kids what to think.

- Label what students do versus what they don't do.

- Provide a chance for students to activate background knowledge and ask questions without penalty or fear of embarrassment for being wrong.

- Provide a variety of text and let students choose which text to read.

- Model a variety of ways to show thinking (avoid fill in the blanks or copying notes).

- Provide clean copies of text so students have room to annotate thinking.

- Provide short, written feedback on students' work to encourage and direct learning.

Table 2.3 (continued)

Long-Term Planning Components that Remove the Masks

The key to long-term planning is anticipating the different masks that learners may come to class wearing. Surely there will be at least one kid who acts silly or sullen to avoid the work. There will be some who act bored and others who respond well to personal attention. Count on at least a few students arriving wearing the mask of anger. Be ready for their question, "Why do we have to know or do this?"

On the left-hand side of this chart, I brainstorm possibilities that cause students to disengage. On the right-hand side, I pair planning structures I can use to influence student engagement and learning.

Possible Causes of Disengagement	Long-Term Planning Structures to Address Disengagement
Students don't see a reason to learn the material	Compelling reasons to study a **Topic**
Students have to guess what the end goal is	Provocative questions tied to the **Topic** or the **Task**
Feedback comes too late	Long-term **Targets** and identified big **Tasks** that exist in the world
Some students need more scaffolding than others	Daily **Tasks** or makes tied to minilessons that drive daily engagement towards long-term targets
Students can't read the assigned text	Choice of accessible **Text** and strategy instruction to read complex text

Table 2.4

Compelling Reasons to Study the Topic

In anticipation of students who wear the mask of boredom or anger, who complain that "this is so stupid," I flesh out compelling reasons why the topic matters. If students know why the unit of study is important, they are more interested in sharing the workload. If I've done a good job articulating the big ideas of my content and unit then students ten years from now will remember the study. To do this, I must provide a real-world connection and purpose to the learning. I don't go out of my way to share these reasons with students or make a big to-do about them. Instead, I have them ready and waiting for the student who says, "Why do I have to learn this?"

Provocative Questions That Invite Students to Read, Write, and Discuss

No one gets too excited about trying to guess what's in someone's head by answering a question that already has an answer. Powerful questions that pique interest and provoke thinking give students a reason to read, write, and talk. For each unit, I design four or five open-ended questions rife with controversy that connect to the topic. Some educators might call them guiding or essential questions. I call them *provocative* questions because their purpose is to provoke students to read, write, and discuss. I post them in the room so students and I can refer to them. They also serve to help students determine what to read, write, and discuss to get smarter about the topic.

Long-Term Targets Connected to the Standards

When planning, I keep in mind that I'm not teaching the standards. I want students to meet and exceed them. I don't plan units by ticking off each standard as I go. Instead, I select the reading and writing standards that connect best with the topic, making sure I address all standards over the course of a year. I don't address every standard in every unit. Some lend themselves to depth in different ways depending on the topic and the genre I'm asking students to read and write.

Once I've identified the standards, I create three or four long-term targets that will help students meet and exceed them. Next, I add supporting targets that serve as rungs on a ladder that students can use as they climb toward proficiency.

Imagine a standard as a high dive platform that we want students to reach. They don't simply reach that platform by flying to the top because we've covered a standard. Students need a way to progress to the platform. Supporting targets are steps in a ladder that help students reach the top. Not every student is going to start at the same place on the ladder. And because some students may be stronger or have longer legs, they may not have to use each rung or climb at the same rate.

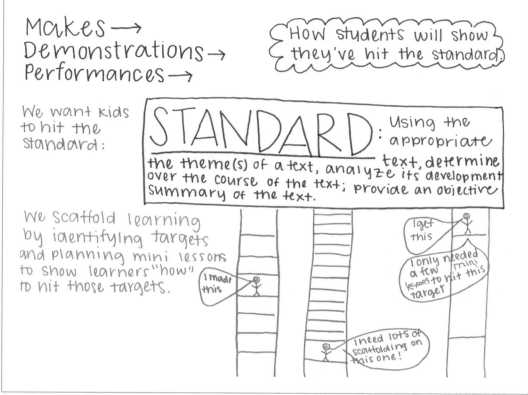

Illustration by Caroline Tovani

Figure 2.2
Platform Drawing of Targets Connected to the Standards

Long-term learning targets should connect to the standards and serve as a path to guide teachers and students. When teachers clearly identify what they want students to know and be able to do, it gives learners a destination and something on which they can reflect. Well-written targets help teachers design minilessons, create flexible instructional groups, and construct summative assessments that give students a way to demonstrate that they've hit the standard.

Long-term targets are posted in the classroom on brightly colored paper above the white board in my room. They are visible so that both the teacher and students can refer to them during minilessons, work time, and conferences. Students can refer to the targets to reflect on what they know and need as they move toward hitting the standard.

Supporting Targets Connected to Daily Needs

As I mentioned earlier, supporting targets are like rungs on a ladder that help students reach the standards at the end of the unit. These targets vary from week to week depending on students' needs. Supporting targets scaffold the different needs of learners in the classroom. Just as there is no perfect minilesson that will meet the needs of all students, there is no perfect supporting target. Because kids are in different places, I think about which targets will support the most students. Weekly targets are listed on the board. Typically, I have three listed, because students are in different places and have different needs. The whole-class minilesson is directed at the target that I think will help the greatest number of students. After the minilesson, students decide which target they are going to work toward for that day. During conferences and small-group instruction, I can check in with students to assess understanding and notice patterns of confusion, which will help me while planning the following day's minilesson.

Big and Little Makes and Do's (Summative and Formative Assessments) Connected to Learning Targets

For long-term and supporting targets to be effective, students need a way to demonstrate that they've hit the target. This is where the tasks come into play. If I've written a solid learning target, there should be a matching task. This task serves as an assessment to help me see what students know and need next. I think of big makes and do's as summative assessments and little makes and do's as formative assessments.

Providing Choice of Accessible Text and Strategy Instruction to Read Complex Text

If I want all readers to grow, I need to have a variety of text at the ready. Text sets should represent diverse voices and perspectives as well as different text structures that range in levels of complexity. Often I will include a complex anchor text in a unit, giving me an opportunity to mentally model how to read and access information. This text gives students an opportunity to see different ways to construct meaning. I also look for texts that will give students choices in how they build their background knowledge. I try to provide text on the topic that accommodates the different reading levels, cultures, and perspectives of students represented in the room. I want to give students opportunities not only to practice using thinking strategies to improve their comprehension, but also to build their background knowledge on how to read different text structures. The more variety, the better. I look for picture books, articles, and primary documents. I collect photos, info-graphics, charts and graphs, lyrics, poetry—any text that can be found in the world outside of school that will give students context as they build their background knowledge, develop vocabulary, and increase comprehension skills.

Throughout the book you will notice stories describing different CYA structures I've used. As you read the different examples, it might seem overwhelming. I don't ever plan to use all the CYA structures at once, but rather, I use them to address the diverse needs of students who enter my classroom. No one planning structure works for all kids. Play with those I've shared, and see which of them work for you.

There are so many things that I wish I would have known twenty years ago. But that's the beauty of teaching—we can always get better for kids. For years, I focused and survived using mostly two Ts: **Tend to me** and **Text**. I worked hard to build relationships with kids and a lot of the time, I did find great text. But there were so many more engagement structures I could have used. No wonder I was so tired!

In the following chapters, I will share with you what I wished I would have known years ago. We will take a closer look at the different ways disengaged students show up to class. We will examine how both unit-based and daily CYA structures can affect their behavioral, emotional, and cognitive engagement. Some-times the first strategy I tried worked. Other times it took me several strategies to pry off the mask. No single CYA strategy works all the time. Figuring out the masks kids are wearing and what each student might need to show their true selves, makes our job incredibly difficult but also wildly rewarding. Let's begin with a few stories about students who wear the masks of anger and apathy . . .

Chapter 3
The Masks of Anger and Apathy

*We must not see any person as an abstraction. Instead
we must see within every person a universe with its own
secrets, with its own treasures, with its own sources of
anguish, and with some measure of triumph.*

—Elie Wiesel, in his foreword to The Nazi Doctors and the Nuremburg Code by
George J. Annas and Michael A. Grodin

The Mask of Anger

It's the first day of school. Students enter the room and begin scanning the tables
to see where to sit. I walk over to a group of five students, three girls and two boys
who have already commandeered their space. One of the boys is perched on the
corner with his back to me. I ask him his name. Without looking up, he tells me
it's Stephen. I say to the table, "Can you all move over a little bit so Stephen has
room to sit on the side? That way he'll have some work space and he won't have to
hurt his neck looking at the screen."

Stephen looks up with a glare and barks at me, "I was Ms. Wooster's student
assistant last semester. She loves me and I can sit anywhere I want. If you want to
kick me out because of where I'm sitting, that's fine. Just do it."

Taken aback by his response and not wanting to get into a power struggle during
the first five minutes of class, I wonder what Stephen is so angry about. "That's
fine," I say. "Of course I don't want to kick you out. You can sit wherever you want.
I was just worried that you didn't have a space to work and that your neck would
get sore twisting around to see the screen."

I smile, and as I walk away, I hear Stephen tell Camy, "Move over so I can see."
Stephen scooches his chair around to claim his space.

Angry kids can be scary, but I'm always surprised how far a little tenderness can
go. After this initial encounter, Stephen lightens up. Later that day, Ms. Wooster,

the assistant principal, affirms that he is a master at getting into power struggles so he can get kicked out of class. Stephen writes like a first grader. He hates to read, probably because he can't decode many of the words. No wonder he comes to English wearing the mask of anger.

The Mask of Apathy

It's day one of a two-day demonstration lesson with an eighth-grade social studies class. I have been asked to introduce the causes of the American Civil War and model some ways for students to hold their thinking as they read the textbook. Anticipating that there will be some kids in the class who aren't reading at grade level, I bring a variety of text that students can choose to read. I also anticipate that some may not know how to "talk back" to their reading, so I plan to model different ways I interact with text. Additionally, I want students to have options for how they show their new thinking, so I model how to use the two-column thinksheet. For more on thinksheets, see Chapter 6 and Appendix B. I have two days with these students. I craft the following learning targets and share them in the opening of the lesson. I want students to have a heads-up of where we are going so we can own the goals together:

- I can define what a civil war is.

- I can describe "tipping point" events of the American Civil War.

- I can explain how enslavement impacts an economy and the individuals who are enslaved.

- I can ask questions I care about.

After I do the minilesson and kids are released to read and write, I start to confer. I head to Mack's table and notice that he is doodling on his notebook. I compliment his artistic ability and ask him what he has chosen to read. Under his breath, he makes a comment. I don't hear it, but his tablemates laugh nervously. Instead of asking him to repeat what he said, I select the piece of text that I think is the most intriguing. There are few words on it, but there are several photos taken in the 1860s. Accompanying the photos are charts and graphics comparing slavery of the past to slavery today.

To check Mack's ability to decode, I ask him to read a line, *Modern day Slavery is more prevalent today than it was in the 1800s.* He decodes beautifully. I then point to the pictures.

"Which one grabs your attention?" I ask. He points to a photo of pre–Civil War workers harvesting cotton. I nod. "That picture disturbs me. What does it make you think?"

With disdain, he asks, "Why do white people ask black and brown people to do things they could do for themselves?"

I nod my head again. "Yep, that's a great question. Seems like it might still be happening. I wonder if studying the past will help us better understand what's going on today?"

Mack looks at me. "Maybe."

"Do you think you could keep reading and add one or two questions to your sheet?"

Mack responds, "Maybe." His table gets quiet as they start to read and I walk away.

After the demo, several teachers give me the skinny on Mack. "He never does work," one says.

Another one leans in and whispers, "When he was in my class, he just sat there."

His current teacher explains, "He moved to our school midyear, and I'm his second social studies teacher. So far we are getting along fine, but he doesn't really participate."

Bless those teachers for trying to make me feel better. But I wasn't the one who mattered. Gently pulling back Mack's mask of apathy was what mattered.

Apathetic kids can be frustrating, but I'm always surprised how far a little honest modeling of thinking can go. That afternoon, as I look at the work that students left me, I see Mack's sticky note that reads, *I have zero questions.* I chuckle.

"Oh, he has questions," I mutter to myself, "just not ones he thinks I can handle." Of course Mack didn't care about something that happened so long ago. And why should he care about it when such awful civil rights violations are occurring right now?

That night, I decide to model some of my thinking for Mack to see the next day. I pull out my own set of stickies and go to town. I start with "Here's what I wonder . . ."

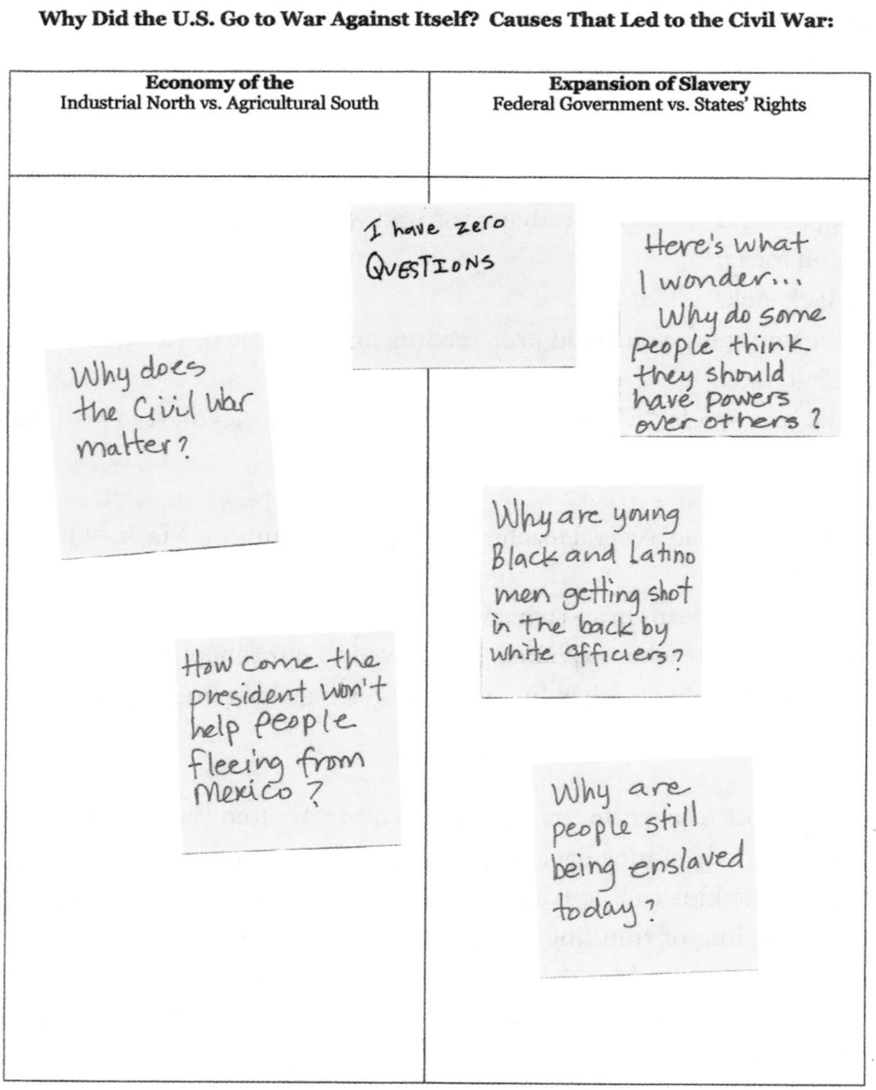

Why Did the U.S. Go to War Against Itself? Causes That Led to the Civil War:

Economy of the Industrial North vs. Agricultural South	Expansion of Slavery Federal Government vs. States' Rights

I have zero QUESTIONS

Here's what I wonder... Why do some people think they should have powers over others?

Why does the Civil War matter?

Why are young Black and Latino men getting shot in the back by white officers?

How come the president won't help people fleeing from Mexico?

Why are people still being enslaved today?

Figure 3.1
Mack's "I Have Zero Questions" Sticky

> ### Modeling MY Questions on Sticky Notes (Task)
>
> - Why do some people think they should have power over others?
> - Why are young Black and Latino men getting shot in the back by white police officers?
> - Why does the Civil War matter?
> - How come the president won't help people fleeing from Mexico?
> - Why are people still enslaved today?

Not all of my questions connected directly to the causes of the Civil War. My goal was to jolt Mack out of his apathy by modeling some questions that weren't too "teachery." If I don't first connect to Mack on a personal level and model that I care about his thinking, he's not going to take a risk that could lead to embarrassment. I also have to help him connect the past to current events. Going after history from 150 years ago without some context or connection to the present can make anyone apathetic.

I think about the mask Mack is wearing. Why did he feign apathy? Was it because he didn't know what I wanted him to do? Was it because he didn't think I'd care about his questions? Was it because I was white and he was Latino?

It's so easy to ignore kids who act apathetic when there are so many other kids in class vying for attention. Even with my authentic, provocative, and personal questions, I didn't hook Mack that second day. He wrote a few more things on his thinksheet but nothing to brag about. If I had a few more days of modeling, pushing back, and figuring out what made him tick, I bet I could've hooked him.

Over the last thirty years, I've met a lot of kids who use the masks of anger and apathy to avoid failure, struggle, reading, and writing. Unfortunately, their masks are effective in that they repel a lot of teachers. The masks help them play their role so well that we are convinced this is who they are all the time. In reality, these masks of anger and apathy give students a way to hide and cover up their academic insecurities and how they really feel.

Teacher as Chief Connector

Before I can get kids to dig into content, first I have to dig into what makes them tick. The very first day of class, I work to connect with students. I want to know them as learners and as human beings. Before I meet my students, I take a stab at the first task I'm planning to assign: to write a letter telling me about themselves so I can better meet their needs.

Before I even start writing, I realize that asking students to tell me about themselves might be a recipe for disaster. Surely, in a class of thirty-one, I'll have some kids who have no idea how to start. Others might be unclear about what they should share. I ask myself, *What would I need if someone asked me to write a letter about myself?* I would wonder what they wanted to know. *Do they care about me as a teacher, a pickle ball player, a mom? Do they want to know what I like and dislike? Do they want to know what kind of wine I drink or where I like to dine?* You get the point. Just asking kids to write a letter about themselves is too broad.

I grab a blank piece of paper and jot down a few things I want to know about them. As I write my own letter, questions start to pop into my head. I write a few down that I hope will entice them to push back or think out of the box. I want to know how I can best help them succeed and why they might not have been successful in other classes. Instead of the letter being a surface, introductory activity, the task will now serve as a quick formative assessment to help me better serve my students. I type up the questions so they are ready to distribute when the first kid asks, "So, what am I supposed to write about?"

In your letter, here are some things you could tell me:

- *What do you like/dislike about reading and writing?*

- *When it comes to school, what's hard for you?*

- *When it comes to school, what's easy for you?*

- *What works for you as a learner?*

- *What do you like to do for fun?*

- *How do you want to get smarter during the first two weeks of school?*

- *What should I know about you to do the best job I can?*

- *What would you hate for your last English teacher to know about you?*

Before I assign the letter task to students, I show my letter to them. I tell them a little bit about myself and what to expect from the class. I make myself vulnerable by sharing how learning hasn't always been easy for me. I explain that I struggled as a reader and that my tenth-grade English teacher told me not to even bother applying to college, that I'd be lucky to graduate. Being vulnerable often helps me connect with others, especially kids who feel angry, apathetic, threatened, or afraid. The letter gives them a little taste of my personality and some insight into what to expect. I hope it sets the tone that this class is going to be more than just learning about nouns and verbs.

Dear Readers, Writers, and Activists,

I'm so happy you are here! I already admire you for making it to first hour on time. Our year will go by fast. In order for me to do the best job I can, I'd like to tell you a little bit about myself, and then I'd like to know a little bit about you.

I love being a teacher, and I want you to be successful. So, that means I will do everything I can to help you learn. I won't trick you. I won't make you feel dumb. I will show you how to do something and I will give you lots of chances to do it well.

I used to be a fake reader and didn't think I could write very well. I had lots of ways to cheat and get out the work. Many teachers didn't believe in me and I almost gave up trying to improve my reading and writing. Over the last thirty years, I've tried hard to learn how to be a better teacher of reading and writing so that kids wouldn't feel bad like I did. I will show you what I learned so that you will be better at reading and writing and maybe even like it a little more.

I will teach you how to use reading and writing strategies that will help you get unstuck. These strategies will help you with any kind of reading and writing you do. I will provide tools that will help you record "snippets" of thinking as you read so that you can use your learning to talk and write about important issues.

When it comes to a grade, I want you all to get As. Below are three behaviors that will enable you to be successful in this class and hopefully in life, as well:

- Show up.
- Try new ways of learning, and don't give up on the first try.
- Read the feedback you get and consider doing something about it.

We are going to dig into complex topics. Therefore, I will rarely ask for "one right answer." I want to see and hear your thinking. When you show me what you get and what you don't get, it helps me to be a better teacher for you.

I will give you feedback so you can revise, redo, and rethink your work. For me, revising thinking is the most important aspect of learning. My goal is that every day you get smarter.

Don't worry. I won't surprise you with quizzes and tests. I won't make you read aloud, and I won't embarrass you. During our time together, we will do lots of reading, writing, and talking. I will show you how, but not what, to think. You will have lots of opportunities to practice and figure things out. We will all get smarter together!

You are going to rock it!

Cris Tovani

Kids walk into the classroom on the first day of school; they are quiet, assessing the lay of the land. Some ask me where to sit and I say, "Wherever you'd like." Six boys rush to sit at a table that is meant for four. Not looking in their direction, I say, "Make sure that there are only four people at a table. If there are more, grab a new seat or I'll find one for you." Two boys begrudgingly move to nearby seats.

Once students get settled I tell them my name and that I'm glad they are here. I see a few eye rolls and heads bending down to check phones hidden under the table. As I pass out the letter, I explain that I wrote them a note that I hope will make them feel better about being back at school. I invite them to read it and encourage them to jot down any thoughts in the margins that they want to remember. While they are reading, I circulate the room, hoping to gain some insight into their thinking by reading the comments they have written.

Most of them finished quickly, and only a few wrote anything in margins. I can tell they didn't read the whole thing. I announce to the class that if anyone is bored reading my note, that's fine. They don't have to read the whole thing. However, I suggest they might want to read the bottom half of the letter, as this will tell them how I'm going to grade. I see a few heads bend down to read. After another minute, I ask if any of them read like I used to. "Anyone in here a fake reader?" A few heads look my way. "Yeah, I was great at that," I say. "When I get to know you better, I will tell you how I did it and why I didn't love school." A few more students return to their letters. After another minute, I ask students to turn to each other and share anything that strikes them. Most kids don't talk, but I wait, knowing that as much as I hate wait time, students hate it more. I can tell that today will be a game of chicken to see who can out-wait the other.

After about fifteen seconds of silence, Caleb, asks, "So what do we call you?"

"You can call me Cris, you can call me Tovani, or Ms. Tovani." Then I laugh and say, "Just don't call me a bad name. I might cry."

Caleb looks at me suspiciously and says, "You really don't care if I call you Cris?"

"No, that's my name."

"So, Cris, were you really bad at school?"

"I wasn't really bad," I say, "I just was really good at cheating and getting out of work." I can tell that I've gotten a few people's attention with that comment. "We don't have a lot of time to fake it in this class. And because of that, I want you to be honest about what you need to get smarter." As I answer Caleb's question, I pass out clean pieces of paper. "You've seen my letter. Now, it's your chance to write one."

Before I can even finish my thought, someone blurts out, "What do you want us to write?"

I smile and say, "I thought someone might be wondering about that." I walk over to the counter and pick up the handout with possible suggestions. "Here is a list of things I'm curious to know. If you are stuck and don't know what to write, this list might give you some ideas. If there are things you think I should know, don't worry about answering my questions. You decide what you want to share to help me do a better job for you." About a third of the class gets up and walks over to the counter to get the list. The others start to write.

Later that morning, the assistant principal, Ms. Wooster, drops by to see how the class is going. I notice her talking to Caleb and smiling. I meet with her in the afternoon, and she asks me about Caleb. I tell her that the first day was rough, but it will get better. She chuckles and says, "He can be really challenging but I think you got him."

"What do you mean?" I ask.

"Caleb is infamous for putting teachers through the ringer," she says. "But when you told him he could call you by your first name, he decided he'd give you a chance."

I let out a sigh. "What about Stephen?" I ask. I tell Ms. Wooster what he said about being her student assistant and that he told me he could sit anywhere he wanted.

She laughs and says, "He's another one who would rather fight than read. The best thing you can do with him is avoid a power struggle, show him what to do, and give him positive feedback."

Recognizing the different masks kids wore that day helped me dodge a couple of bullets. It never occurred to me that giving kids slack on where they sat or how they referred to me was a big deal. I realized that a little tenderness and vulnerability saved me. I let out a sigh and thought about all the unintentional consequences that occur in the name of power and control. Thank goodness I didn't instigate a power struggle over Stephen's seat or insist on Caleb calling me Ms. Tovani. If there's going to be a hill I die on, I'm glad it wasn't one of those.

That afternoon, I dig into the letters that students wrote. I quickly notice that there is a wide range of readers and writers sitting in the room. I read Caleb's first. No wonder he finished so fast. He only wrote two sentences. From his letter, I learn that he thinks reading and writing are boring and he likes to talk. I also notice that he likes to take pictures. I ask him a question, and the following day he responds with an answer.

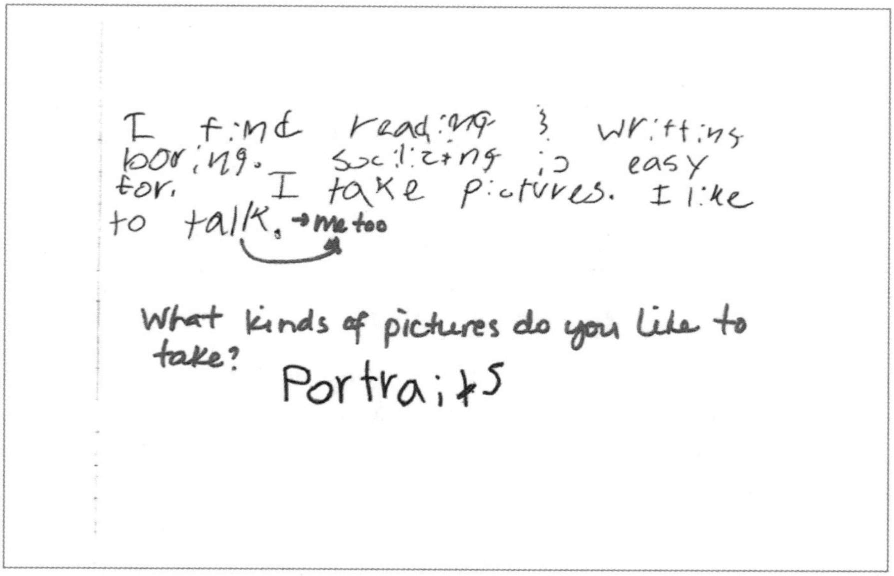

I find reading & writting boring. Socilizing is easy for. I take pictures. I like to talk. → Me too

What kinds of pictures do you like to take? Portraits

Figure 3.2
Caleb's First Day Letter

Next, I read Vanessa's letter. I learn a lot more about her. She doesn't like to read because her mind wanders. From this comment, I gather that she needs to know how to monitor her comprehension and have some ways to "talk back" to text. I can definitely help her in those areas. I also learn that getting to school is hard for her. Questions start to pop into my head. *Is she late because of a transportation issue? Does she stay up too late at night so waking up early in the morning is hard? Did she get bored with her past first-hour classes and decide sleeping in was more rewarding?*

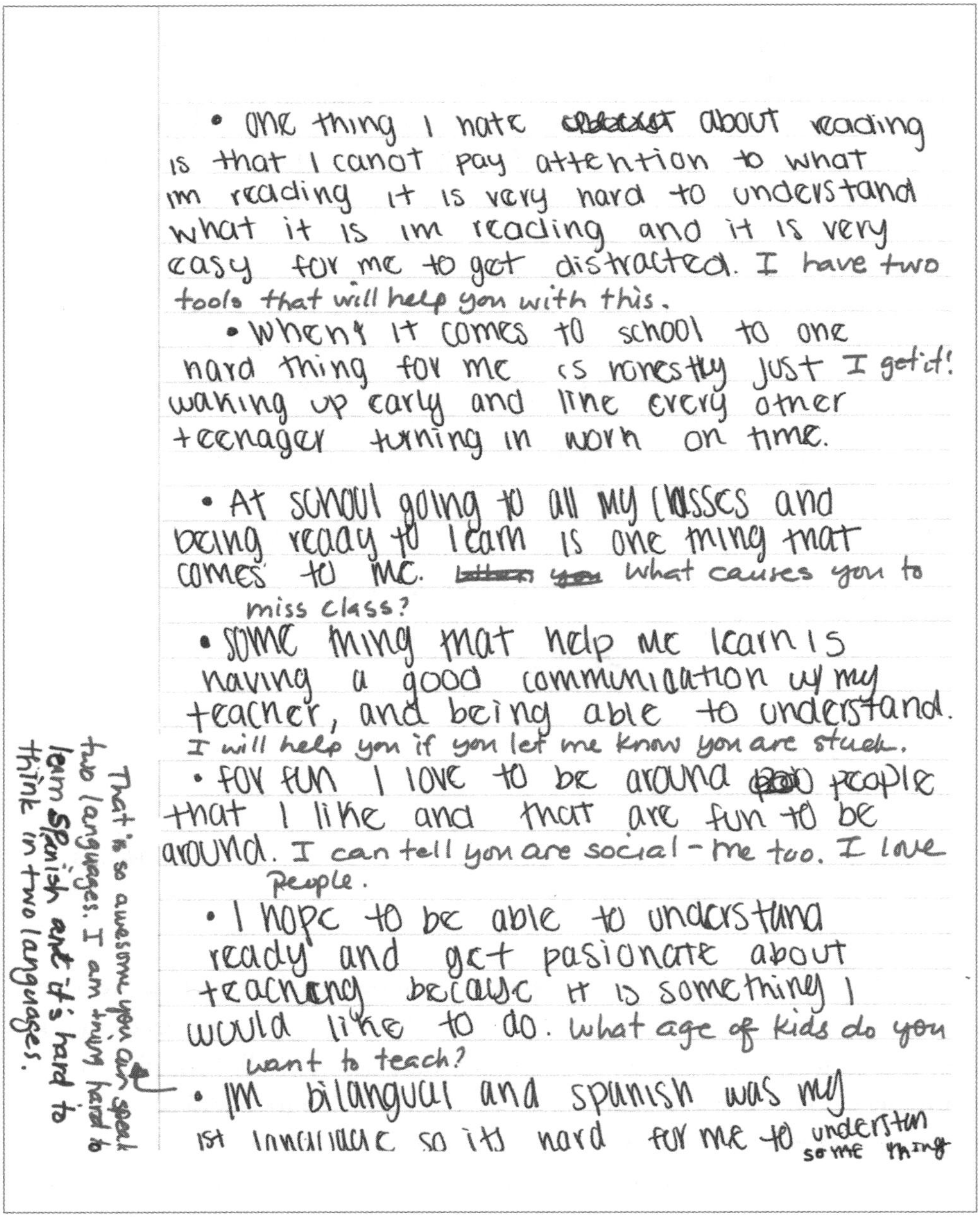

• One thing I hate ~~aladadst~~ about reading is that I canot pay attention to what im reading it is very hard to understand what it is im reading and it is very easy for me to get distracted. I have two tools that will help you with this.

• When it comes to school to one hard thing for me is honestly just *I get it!* waking up early and line every other teenager turning in work on time.

• At school going to all my classes and being ready to learn is one thing that comes to me. ~~llars you~~ *What causes you to miss class?*

• Some thing that help me learn is having a good communication w/ my teacher, and being able to understand. *I will help you if you let me know you are stuck.*

• For fun I love to be around ~~people~~ people that I like and that are fun to be around. *I can tell you are social - me too. I love people.*

• I hope to be able to understand ready and get pasionate about teaching because it is something I would like to do. *what age of kids do you want to teach?*

• Im bilanguci and spanish was my 1st lancuuac so its hard for me to understan *some thing*

That's so awesome you can speak two languages. I am trying hard to learn Spanish and it's hard to think in two languages.

Figure 3.3
Vanessa's First Day Letter

Vanessa goes on to write, "Something that helps me learn is having good communication with my teacher and being able to understand." I wonder what that means. *Maybe she is afraid to ask teachers questions. Maybe she doesn't know how to isolate her confusion by asking questions. Maybe she doesn't even know when she is confused.* Reading on, I learn that socializing is important to Vanessa and that someday she wants to be a teacher. In the last paragraph, she tells me she is bilingual and that Spanish is her first language. She goes on to write that ". . . it's hard for me to understand some things." Maybe as she is translating from Spanish to English, she misses new instructions or needs more time to process. Perhaps that's why it is sometimes hard for her to understand.

Knowing that Vanessa moves between two languages alerts me that I will need to check in with her to see if she needs more time to complete the task, or if she needs directions repeated or written down. I will also need to regularly check to see what she understands. If I can help her advocate for herself by asking questions, it will make my job easier. I write a few notes to her, starting with the reminder to honor that she can speak in two languages and that being bilingual is an asset.

The last letter I read is Karissa's. I think she told me earlier in the day that her parents migrated to the United States from Russia when she was four. I wonder if she is also an English learner, like Vanessa? I notice that Karissa is one of only a few students who has closely followed the format of my letter. She admits right off the bat that she is a horrible speller. This isn't demonstrated in her writing, but maybe she's been taught to put a high value on accurate spelling. She tells me that school can be a struggle for her if it gets boring or if she finds something better to do. She also has to like the environment. I wonder if she means what the room looks like or how she is treated by the teacher and other students? She admits that if conditions aren't to her liking, she won't come to class. I'm grateful for Karissa's honesty. I infer from what she has written that she seeks relevance, an environment conducive to learning, and collaboration with the teacher and other students.

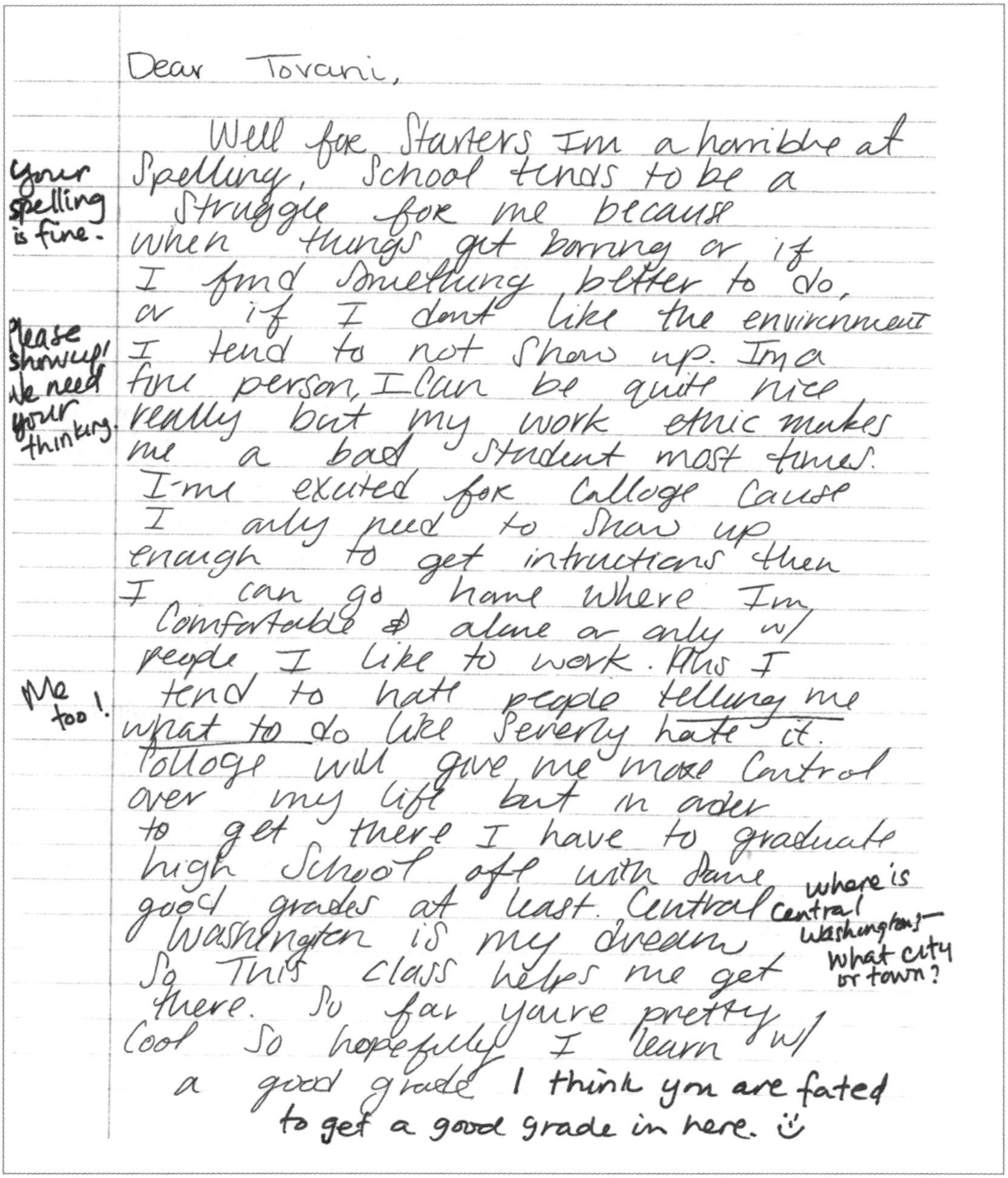

Dear Tovani,

Well for Starters Im a horrible at Spelling, School tends to be a Struggle for me because when things get borring or if I find Something better to do, or if I dont like the environment I tend to not Show up. Im a fine person, I can be quite nice really but my work ethic makes me a bad Student most times. I'me excited for College cause I only need to Show up enough to get intructions then I can go home where I'm Comfortable & alone or only w/ people I like to work. Plus I tend to hate people telling me what to do like Severly hate it. College will give me more Control over my life but in order to get there I have to graduate high School off with some good grades at least. Central Washington is my dream So This class helps me get there. So far youre pretty cool So hopefully I learn w/ a good grade I think you are fated to get a good grade in here. ☺

Margin notes:
Your spelling is fine.

Please show up! We need your thinking.

Me too!

where is Central Washington — what city or town?

Figure 3.4
Karissa's First Day Letter

Reading Karissa's letter, I was struck by the tone. I noticed that she underlined, "I hate people telling me what to do."

Who doesn't? I thought. I also translated this into her wanting to have some choice in what she reads, does, and thinks. Karissa writes that she wants to go to college and in order to do that, she has to graduate. I inferred that she wants me to know that she will play along if I keep her engaged with interesting and challenging work.

After reading the letters, I started to make a list of what students need:

Caleb needs to increase the minutes he reads and writes every day. That is priority number one. Next, I need to connect him with short and engaging text. Since he doesn't write very much, I will give him feedback on anything he does write to keep him going. I need to honor his need to talk but model how to use reading and listening as a way to enhance what he has to say.

Vanessa needs multiple opportunities to hear instructions. Instructions that require multiple steps might need to be written down for her to reference. I need to help her realize that good readers and writers ask questions when they don't understand. I want to model for her how to identify confusion and feel comfortable asking for help.

Karissa needs choice. This could be choice in what she writes or how she shows her thinking. I need to help her understand the purpose behind the work she is doing. I can do this by sharing compelling reasons why the work matters and how the work connects to her life. I want to challenge her to think in new ways and watch for signs of boredom.

Connecting Kids to Content

It doesn't matter if I'm teaching a room full of kids who have been with me all year or if I'm doing a two-day demo with brand new students, I have to assess what they know and care about in terms of the topic or unit I am introducing. It doesn't frustrate me when students don't have a lot of background knowledge about a topic because it gives me the chance to create curiosity. When kids are curious, it drives them to read, write, and talk.

When we began our unit on refugees using Syria as a case study, Caleb told me that he knew nothing about Syria, "zero, zilch, nada." He wasn't the only one in the room. I didn't know much about the Syrian refugee crisis either until I started planning the unit. To be honest, the conflict and problems plagued by the Syrian civil war are so complex that I'll never fully understand. But because of this unit, I am a more informed citizen who can use the information to make decisions about how I vote and interact with people who are different from me.

In John Hattie and Gregory Yates's book, *Visible Learning and the Science of How We Learn* (2014,114), the authors discuss different ways we acquire and retain information. They emphasize the power of prior knowledge stating, "The single most important factor influencing learning is what the learner already knows."

Our students do not always come to us with the background knowledge we would like them to have. A reader's background knowledge can powerfully influence their comprehension of complex text. I keep this in mind as I plan. When I begin a unit, the first order of business is to assess and build students' background knowledge as quickly and as painlessly as possible. Lecturing about a topic can be deadly, so I gather images, quotes, statistics, and excerpts of compelling text that connect to the topic. I cut, arrange, and paste them on tabloid size paper (11 by 17 inches) and call them Background Knowledge Placemats.

These Background Knowledge Placemats give me a way to see where kids are starting in their thinking. As students read and view the choices of text, some will complain they don't know anything about the images in front of them, so they can't make any connections. When good readers lack background knowledge, they ask questions. Therefore, students can also respond by sharing what they wonder as they read the Background Knowledge Placemats. Their questions help me assess what they know, discover misconceptions, find out what they are curious about, and gain insight into what they care about.

For Caleb's and Stephen's class, I share the placemats on the second day of the unit. When students enter the room, they find a "placemat" of images and texts on their table. Each table has a different placemat.

"What the heck is this?" shouts Caleb.

"That poor kid. Is he in shock?" asks Vanessa.

"I've heard of barrel bombs, but didn't know what they were," admits Stephen.

"Can't you see they are at war?" snaps Camy.

The fact that students are already drawn to the images is a good sign—it tells me I've chosen compelling text and graphics for them to study. As students settle into their seats, I instruct them to grab two sticky notes and a Background Knowledge Placemat from the center of the table.

"Study the images," I say, "and if you want to read the words on the page, that's great. The words and captions might give you more information or cause you to have more questions." Giving students a choice to read the accompanying words versus telling them to "be sure and read the words" gives them agency. Often the kids who read the text will point out to their peers that the words actually help them understand what is going on in the photo or graphic.

"On one of your sticky notes," I say, "write what you think you get about the pictures in front of you. On the other sticky note, write something you are wondering about."

"Then what do we do with the sticky notes?" asks Johnny. "Do we put our name on them?"

"If you wrote something smart, put your name on the sticky. If you don't know if it's smart, you can leave your name off." This gives students the opportunity for self-reflection.

"But where do I put the stickies?" repeats Johnny.

"Put the sticky note next to the place where you have the thinking," I explain. "That way, the next table group can see your thoughts and maybe add to it."

"What? People are going to read what I write?" asks Caleb.

"If it's interesting, they will. If it's silly or boring, they probably won't."

"So, what do we write?" asks Caleb.

"Write to a picture that strikes you. Explain what you think you get about it or ask a question that you care about. Don't read the whole placemat unless you want to, just read the parts that grab you." Once again, when students are given the choice of where and what they read, they tend to read more than when I order them to read the whole thing. If no one reads, it's a signal that I didn't select provocative enough pictures and text.

As students begin to study their placemats, building background knowledge and curiosity, I start to study them. I watch to see what they write. I listen to them talk about the text. I notice who is interested in the reading but not necessarily interested in recording their thinking. Sometimes I stop and ask, "What do you think about this picture?" and then scribe what they say on a sticky note. I want students to understand that I'm looking to see thinking, not for right answers.

After three or four minutes, depending on the students' interest and endurance, I call time and ask them to rotate clockwise to the next table. "This time," I instruct, "you not only have new images and text to read, but you can also respond to your classmates' thoughts."

Sitting down at the next table, Stephen says, "What's wrong with this kid?"

I head to his table and ask him what he's reading. He points to the now famous photo of shell-shocked five-year-old Omran Daqneesh, sitting in an ambulance with dust, blood, and a blank stare on his face.

I explain to Stephen just loud enough for others at the table to hear, "This little boy is one of thousands of children whose homes have been bombed. He was lucky enough to survive. Did you see the letter below the picture?"

Stephen and the other four at the table shift their gaze to a letter written to President Barack Obama from a six-year-old named Alex. Alex had seen the images of Omran on television and wrote his letter asking if President Obama could please find "the boy who was picked up by the ambulance in Syria" and bring him to his house so that his family could take care of him.

"How did that little boy find out about the boy in Syria?" asks Camy.

Pointing to Omran, Stephen wonders, "Where is that little boy's family?"

"Write those questions down you two," I say, "They are good ones because you are curious about the answers. I don't know the answers to either of your questions, but it makes me wonder if there are a bunch of orphans in Syria? I also wonder how come a six-year-old knew about the kids in Syria and I didn't."

Stephen looks at me with surprise when he realizes that I'm not answering his question. I shrug my shoulders. He looks down and starts to read the letter from Alex.

Virtual Background Knowledge Placemats

For an example of a Virtual Background Knowledge Placemat see pages 207 and 208.

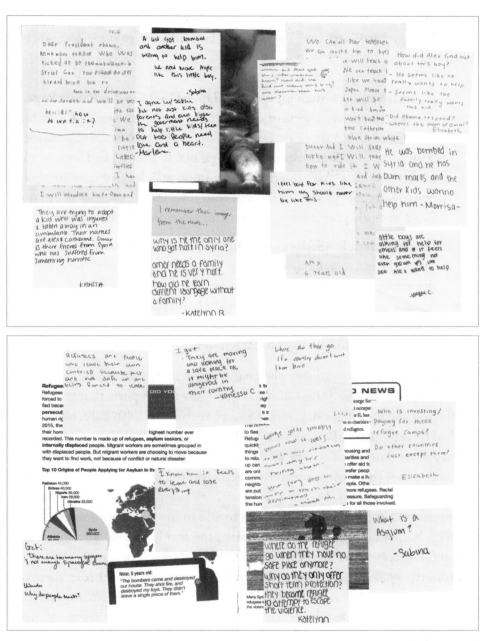

Figure 3.5
Examples of Background Knowledge Placemats

People often ask me, "Where do you find all of this text?" When creating Background Knowledge Placemats, I'm not very fancy. Here are some places where I find short text:

> **Search Engines Such as: Google, DuckDuckGo, and StartPage.**
> I go to the search engine of choice and type in the topic and then hit "Images." Often there are examples of quotes, pictures, and statistics that I can use. This gives me a starting place. Then I head back to the search engine's "All" and from there I find articles that have images with short captions that kids will read. I verify the sources so I'm not inadvertently putting false information in front of the students.
>
> **Independent Bookstores (nonfiction section for younger students).**
> Next, I head to a bookstore and look for nonfiction text that is written for younger children. Often there are excerpts and pictures that older students can quickly view and read to build their background knowledge. I copy, cut, paste, and cite these images on the tabloid paper so there is room for students to attach their sticky notes.

My bottom line and number one goal is to get more kids reading and writing more minutes of the day. John Guthrie's 2004 research reports that students who read sixty-seven minutes a day, tend to score within the 98th percentile on standardized tests (Guthrie, Perencevich, and Wigfield 2004). This doesn't mean that the sixty-seven minutes has to be all at one time, but it does have to be spent reading text that is at the student's reading level. Over the past two days, Stephen only read about eight minutes. But I'm guessing that's eight more minutes than he read on summer break. My goal is to get him to add to his reading minutes every day. It's a high bar, but if the topic is compelling, the text is accessible, and the task is purposeful, Stephen and the other kids in class will reach this goal.

From the placemat activity, I learned a lot about students. I read their sticky notes and rearranged them on the Background Knowledge Placemats to be read by others. Students surprised me by what they knew. I saw a variety of questions and vulnerabilities. Many students asked *who*, *what*, and *when* questions about what they saw. They needed context.

Ender wants to know the details of what happened to Omran Daqneesh, the little boy in the photo. Other students' questions are more philosophical. Thea wants to know why there is war. From Alyssa's question, "Why are little kids seeing stuff like this?" I couldn't tell if she is wondering why six-year-old Alex was allowed to see the news clip of Omran or if she can't believe Omran witnessed such war scenes. Perhaps she doesn't understand that he is a victim of war. Their questions helped me recognize their misconceptions. I assessed background knowledge gaps and began to think about text I've already collected. Now I need to keep my eyes out for more text that will address their questions and build their background knowledge.

The Background Knowledge Placemats with attached sticky notes hang on the wall and remind us that our questions drive how we build our prior knowledge about a topic. Our goal is not to memorize facts, dates, names, and places; it's to study a real-world problem that can affect how we vote, the health of the economy, and how we respond to an international issue.

Connecting Students to Each Other

Connecting kids to content is one way to help them remove their masks of apathy and anger. Another way is to engender collaborative relationships among class-mates. I share some of the annotations from their placemats in a handout before hanging the placemats on the wall for further study. When creating this handout, my goal is to highlight one annotation from each student. Adding complication, there are lots of sticky notes without names. I infer that the students who wrote their name on their sticky notes are either compliant or are confident in what they wrote. I honor the annotations written by kids who didn't add their names along with the others, so the next time they will be more likely to write their name and own their thinking.

First thing tomorrow, I will hand students the page of their captured annota-tions and instruct them to read at least three responses They usually look for their own annotation and then read an annotation of a friend's thinking. After doing this several times throughout the year, students start to read for quoted annotations that will surprise and grow new thinking. Next, I ask them to respond on the handout to one or two ideas that struck them. After they have written something, students are instructed to stand up and find the classmate they wrote to. Some kids will whine that they don't know who the person is. "Great," I say, "this is your chance to find out." My hope is that they start to direct their thinking to each other and not just me. The list below not only serves to highlight thinkers in the room, but it also serves as a model for students who weren't sure what I wanted.

Thoughts and Questions from Tuesday's Background Knowledge Placemats

- "Where do people go if their country doesn't want them anymore?" **Luis, Katelyn**

- "Children have more humanity than adults." **Eliza**

- "Where is Omran Daqneesh's family?" **Stephen**

- "What happened to Omran Daqneesh?" **Ender**

- "Little kids are dying—how do we fix it? How do we combat the bombings?" **Trenton**

- "Did Obama actually see the letter that Alex wrote?"

- "We must also help parents. The government needs to help kids and teens out too. People need love and a heart." **Marlene**

- "When people have to leave, why do they have to come to America?"

- "America needs to do something for these kids in Syria." **Vanessa**

- "What is asylum?" **Sabina**

- "People voted for Bashar to see a change but he did not keep any promises. People of Syria protested."

- "Bashar is using his power for bad and will hurt and kill his own people with his power."

- "How long has the Syrian crisis gone on?"

- "How hot is it in Syria?" **Caleb**

- "Is Damascus restored or is it still bombed out?"

- "With six million refugees, how come only 10 percent live in camps?" **Mikaela**

- "What are people fleeing from?" **Ender**

- "They used to live in a beautiful place now it's bombed, burned down, and broken to pieces." **Grace**

- "Why isn't there space for everyone who needs help?" **Camy**

- "Where did the parents go?" **Luis**

- "What is the point of destroying all your buildings?" **Arely**

- "Is this bombing stuff still going on today?" **Alyssa**

- "Why is it so hard for countries to help and bring in refugees?" **Carolina**

- "Millions of people have been forced to move out of their homes at the end of the year." **Johnny**

- "I don't understand why people don't feel safe."

- "I know how it feels to leave and lose everything."

- "Why is there so much conflict in the Middle East?" **Karissa**

- "Who is paying for these refugee camps?" **Elizabeth**

- "Why do countries only offer short-term protection? They became refugees to escape the violence." **Katelyn**

When students build background knowledge about each other through what they wonder and think about a topic, it helps them to connect. I insist that they know and refer to each other by name. I want them to know each other's stories so they will take risks and work together. If I can nurture an environment where students trust each other, it increases purposeful talk and collaboration among students. Most importantly, it increases the number of teachers in the room. I don't have to be everywhere at the same time. Students don't have to wait for me to help them. When I taught first grade, the rule was "See three before me." It's a great rule for middle and high school kids too.

I love surprising students with other students' thinking. When I honor their words by posting and giving them credit for smart things they say, I help them build connections to each other. This increases their behavioral, emotional, and cognitive engagement. It also helps them remove their masks of anger and apathy. They want to care— about each other and the world.

Connections to Text

One of the fastest ways to disconnect with a student is to assign them to read a text that is too hard or too boring. We all know this, yet kids are still being told to read text that is above their reading level with little or no context. There isn't an in-service or workshop that goes by where a teacher doesn't ask me, "What do I do about kids who won't read?" I don't always do a terrific job answering that question because there are so many possible reasons.

When I ask students why they don't read in school, here are some of the most common responses:

> *Eventually the teacher will tell me what the reading is about.* Many students have been inadvertently trained to expect us to give them the information. So instead of providing students with opportunities to uncover the content with text, we lecture or tell them the information. Lecturing is more efficient than letting kids construct meaning but it's not more effective when it comes to improving comprehension or learning the material.

> *The words are too hard.* Students quit because they haven't acquired the disciplinary vocabulary needed to comprehend the reading. Often this is because they are only asked to read about the words and not use them to do something. They may memorize definitions but unless they use the words to communicate or construct meaning, they are often forgotten.

> *My mind wanders, and I don't want to go back and reread.* Students aren't taught how to monitor their comprehension as they read. So, when meaning breaks down, they don't know how or why to selectively reread with a purpose as they mentally "talk back" and interact with text.

I'm never going to use this information. Students don't see a purpose for their reading. For kids who don't love to read, they need a reason to read. Many students, especially boys, tell me they will read only if it helps them get better at doing something.

The reading is boring. Students often don't care about topics they have no context for. They need compelling reasons to care. The "boring" comment can also be another way for kids to tell us that the text is too hard. If we want students to construct meaning in our content area, one text alone won't cut it. We have to provide options for the different levels of readers in our class.

There is no reason to read when I can see the movie or copy answers off of someone else. When students are only reading to "guess what's in the teacher's head" or to fill out worksheets with one right answer, it's tempting to take the easy way out. When there is no authentic reason to read, students who aren't grade- or curiosity-driven, rely on strategies like copying off a friend, reading SparkNotes, or just waiting to be told what to write.

What Works Best to Connect Kids to Text?

Unfortunately, there isn't one text or strategy to ensure that all kids will read. Here are five strategies I use to make sure students are comprehending better and building background knowledge about the unit.

1. *Use an Anchor Text to Model Reading Strategies.* I define an *anchor text* as reading material that the whole class gets to experience over time. It can be a novel; a chapter from a work of nonfiction; a complex graphic, word problem, or model; a poem; an essay; an article—anything that gives me a chance to think aloud different ways to construct meaning when reading complex text. My focus when using an anchor text is to show students different ways to access and get through complicated reading without quitting or cheating. When I model a thinking strategy, students can then practice it during work time as they build not only their background

knowledge but also their confidence that they too can read the "hard stuff." There is a lot of controversy circling whole-class texts. For me, an anchor text provides a way to model different strategies to construct meaning of complex text. When using fictional anchor texts, students have lots of nonfiction choices to choose from that will build background knowledge for the unit and novel. When the anchor text is nonfiction, students have novels or firsthand accounts that they can choose to read, to build empathy for the nonfiction content we are reading.

2. ***Choice of Different Text Structures.*** If the anchor text is the hub of the wheel, choice reading with a variety of text structures are the spokes. Anchor texts often require context, and this is where choice reading can fit. Choice drives engagement, and when I consider different text structures connected to my unit, I have multiple entry points to hook kids.

3. ***Let Students Reread.*** When working with apathetic or struggling readers, my focus is on increasing students' time on task. If students have a chance in class to reread, which is often unheard of in content-area classes, they experience more success. I would much rather a student read and understand ten pages of text than fake read fifty pages.

4. ***Find Text That Addresses What Students Care and Wonder About.*** This means I have to give students an opportunity to respond to text so that I can see what interests them and what they are curious about. When a student asks a question, I can use a search engine to find one or two pieces of text that address their curiosity.

5. ***Don't Make Students Read the Whole Thing.*** With fiction, I will sometimes summarize a chapter or portion of a novel to get a kid caught up with his book group. With nonfiction, I might start by having kids read headings and then let them choose the section to read that connects to a question they have. Once again, choice drives engagement and gives kids agency to focus on their learning rather than being hamstrung by a curriculum guide or textbook.

Where Do I Find Text That Kids Will Read?

When I look for text, I keep a few types of readers in mind: a Stephen-type kid who struggles with decoding, a Mack-type kid who dares me to get his attention, an English learner like Vanessa, and last, a student like Karissa who hasn't been pushed or challenged. In addition to finding different levels of text, I also strive to find different text structures

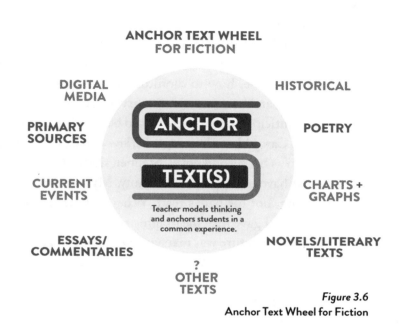

Figure 3.6
Anchor Text Wheel for Fiction

that will provoke and stoke curiosity. When selecting text for students to read, my goal is to find interesting and accessible material that will pull them into the content.

When topics are compelling and connected to a current issue, text is everywhere. If I use lexiles and reading levels as simply tools and I don't handcuff myself to their rigidity, the possibilities of reading materials are vast. Who cares if a student reads something that is below his grade level if it helps him learn about the topic? If teachers have a complex anchor text and model for students how to read it, they not only become better readers, but they will also get smarter about the unit of study.

When I start the search for text, I want to be sure that I include stories that connect to the topic. When students have a chance to learn about the topic and read people's firsthand accounts, apathy soon turns to empathy and students begin to care about the events, people, dates, and facts that envelop the unit. In addition to narratives, I also need nonfiction that represents diverse perspectives so students can build their background knowledge and develop positions on current issues.

When I find a topic that is compelling, interesting text falls into my lap. It's easy to find current events, political cartoons, essays, picture books, novels, poetry, graphics, and historical pieces that readers can choose to read to build their background knowledge. Below is an example of how I organized my text search for the unit on the Syrian refugee crisis. The anchor text was *Refugee* by Alan Gratz. Each student had a copy of the text and it was here that I modeled how to track characters and time, how to monitor comprehension, how to reread with a different purpose, and how to notice literary elements used by the author to convey meaning.

I anticipated that there would be a wide range of reading abilities in the classroom. Camy blasted through *Refugee* and eagerly chose *Escape from Aleppo* by N.H. Senzai as her second novel. Stephen slogged through *Refugee* and felt relief that he didn't have to keep up with Camy. My focus for him was to increase his minutes reading, not his pages read. When I figured out that *Refugee* was too hard for Stephen, I gave him the graphic novel *Escape from Syria* by Samya Kullab to read. The text structure was manageable and it still gave Stephen an opportunity to read stories of refugees and glean information about the Syrian refugee crisis.

Connections Affect Anger and Apathy

Years ago, when colleagues Ellin Keene and Susan Zimmerman wrote their groundbreaking book *Mosaic of Thought* (1997), readers were introduced to thinking strategies used by proficient readers. One of the thinking strategies that skilled readers employ is activating, utilizing, and building background knowledge as a means to making connections.

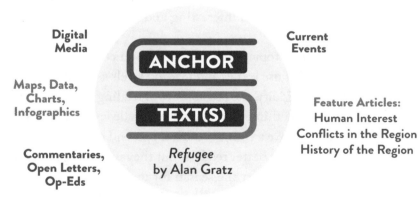

ANCHOR TEXT WHEEL FOR SYRIAN REFUGEE CRISIS

Digital Media

Current Events

Maps, Data, Charts, Infographics

ANCHOR TEXT(S)

Feature Articles: Human Interest Conflicts in the Region History of the Region

Commentaries, Open Letters, Op-Eds

Refugee by Alan Gratz

Novels Connected to the Crisis: *Escape from Aleppo* by N.H. Senzai *Dear World* by Bana Alabed *Escape from Syria* by Samya Kullab

Figure 3.7
Anchor Text Wheel for Syrian Refugee Crisis

As a young teacher, I focused a lot of my instruction on modeling this strategy by helping students make connections to what they knew and what they read. I wasn't the only one who did this. Teachers all over the country were asking kids to share what their reading reminded them of. From kindergarten to high school, students were using the phrase, "This reminds me of . . ." I continued to study metacognition with colleagues such as Stephanie Harvey, Anne Goudvis, Ellin Keene, Debbie Miller, and Samantha Bennett.

As we studied readers of all ages, we learned that just making connections wasn't enough. We had to show students how their connections led to deeper thinking. When students connect, they care about rereading and revising. When students care, it helps them ask questions that can lead to inferences. Connections help readers visualize and empathize. They help students determine importance and go beyond plot or the regurgitation of facts. Connections encourage learners to synthesize thinking and apply it to new learning.

Some literacy leaders diminished the value of teaching readers to make connections because it wasn't something directly assessed. They wrote it off as fluff and complained it was a waste of time because it only made students feel good. Connections do make people feel good. When learners connect with another person, topic, or skill they feel satisfaction. Those who minimize the importance of teaching students how to make connections are partially right. There is nothing in the national standards that says students need to be able to do this. Making connections isn't tested on statewide exams, but teachers who ignore the importance of this strategy do so at their students' risk. The ability to connect leads learners to deeper and more profound learning. Without a connection to a topic, person, purpose, or reason, there is no point in working hard to construct meaning. Life is just too busy!

Connections make us care. The Six Ts provide the following points of connection for angry and apathetic mask-wearers

- a compelling **Topic**

- authentic **Tasks** with related, purposeful **Targets**

- a complex **Task** that will take **Time** and multiple drafts to craft in order to be shared with an authentic audience

- multiple **Texts**

- **Tend**erness offered by the teacher and other classmates

- **Time** to build background knowledge and skills

When student-to-student connections are our motivating force, we plan time to read, write, and talk about engaging topics, to study interesting text, and to work on authentic tasks and purposeful learning goals. This allows students to see relevance and engage in the work they are asked to do.

What Works? Five CYA Strategies That Help Students Take Off the Masks of Anger and Apathy

1. Try a little **Tend**erness by slowing down and taking **Time** to explain why. Remember Stephen: "Of course, I don't want to kick you out. You can sit wherever you want. I was just worried that you didn't have a space to work and that your neck would get sore twisting around to see the screen."

2. **Tend** to students by showing an interest in their lives both inside and outside of school; confer with individuals to learn what interests each of them. Remember the Background Knowledge Placemats: "Which of these pictures grabs your attention? What are you thinking? What else strikes you?"

3. Model the **Task** you want students to engage in. Demonstrate a variety of thinking strategies so students have multiple entry points into text. Help them build a vision for how interesting the world can be. Learners who ask questions they care about, even at the beginning of a **Topic,** build relevancy.

4. Spend planning **Time** reading student work each day, and respond immediately and authentically, using learning **Targets** to guide you. Respond with follow-up questions, connections, and comments that show students their thinking matters most. This practice impacts engagement and achievement because it helps you notice patterns so you can **Target** what students need next.

5. Collect a variety of **Text**—types and perspectives—connected to the issue or topic (narrative, graphs, charts, photographs, primary and secondary sources, infographics, and diagrams) so that students can build their background knowledge about the topic and share what they are curious about.

Chapter 4

The Mask of the Class Clown

We might ask, as a criterion for any subject taught . . . is it worth an adult's knowing and whether having known it as a child makes a person a better adult.

—Jerome Bruner

The first two days of school, Caleb did every annoying thing he could to get kicked out of class. He'd blurt out silly comments and then flash a Cheshire Cat grin my way. When that got old, he asked me questions. "How much money do you make?" "Is that real gold on your watch?" "Are you married?" My one-word answers must have gotten boring, because soon after that, he gave up on me and started whispering annoying comments to the girls at the next table. They were pretty good at ignoring him too, so then he started asking if he could go to the bathroom. On his way there, he pretended to trip, adding a little physical comedy to his repertoire. Upon his return, in no time at all, he organized a video game on his phone with two other students.

Each time Caleb got off task, I'd head over to his table to see what he needed to get back to work. Realizing that he would be the only student I conferred with if I continued with this tactic, I decided to work with kids on the opposite side of the room who hadn't received much attention. For the rest of the period, I watched Caleb on and off, quietly and seriously playing the video game. I think at one point he was engaged for a good twenty-five minutes. His class clown mask was nowhere to be seen. *Hmmm*, I thought, *if he could play a video game for that long, he could probably read and write for that long too.* The trick would be finding something that he would take seriously.

To be honest, Caleb did engage a few times in learning on that first day. He jotted down a couple sentences about who he was as a learner, and he wrote his Instagram handle on his portion of the conversation calendar.

That evening, thinking about Caleb and dreading his antics the next day, I decided to check out his Instagram. Much to my surprise, he had taken some really good photos. Clearly, he doesn't wear the mask of class clown when he's taking photos. I could tell from reading some of the comments that he was serious about photography. Once again, I'm reminded not to judge a kid by the mask he wears in class. This gave me an idea. The next morning, I handed him a beautiful picture book called Where Will I Live? by Rosemary McCarney (2017). The book has limited words, but the pages are filled with stunning, poignant photos of children who have been forced out of their homes for various reasons—violence, climate disaster, war, poverty, and famine.

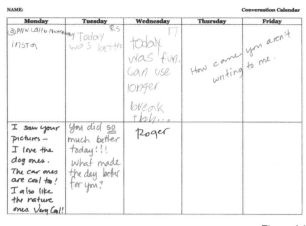

Figure 4.1
Caleb's Conversation Calendar

"Here," I said, offering the book to Caleb. "Check this out. It's pretty cool."

"I'm not reading a baby book."

"Well, you're right, little kids could read this, but the topic is pretty disturbing. Don't read the words, just look at the photos."

"Photos?"

"Yeah, I checked out your Instagram last night and you're pretty good. I thought you might like this book."

"Why, cause you think I can't read?"

"Well, based on the fact that you did very little reading yesterday, I have no idea what kind of reader you are. Since you're a photographer, I just thought you'd appreciate another artist's work. It might give you some ideas about composition, lighting, and background—all that stuff you photographers pay attention to." I set the book on his table and walked away. Caleb's class clown mask came off for fifteen minutes as he pored over the pictures. Glorious silence descended upon the room as kids dug into their reading.

Students who wear the class clown mask aren't doing it to be bad. They want to be successful and taken seriously, but when they struggle, they would rather be perceived as funny than as stupid. When I plan, I anticipate that there will be students who struggle and don't want to read and write. Surely, there will be at least one student like Caleb who jokes around to cover up his reading and writing deficits.

Fortunately, the long-term unit planning I did before I met Caleb's class enabled me to collect lots of engaging texts about refugees through the lens of the Syrian refugee crisis. I armed myself ahead of time with picture books, firsthand accounts, Facebook posts, poetry anthologies, graphic novels, and nonfiction articles that were ready and waiting for students like Caleb.

Over the years, I've figured out the hard way that I have to anticipate different "just right" texts for the different kinds of readers in the room. Thanks to past failures, I've learned lessons that help me do better with the next group of kids I work with.

Why Text Matters

Years ago, I found myself standing in front of twenty-eight science teachers flummoxed. Teachers from around the district had been released for the day to observe me teach reading in a science class. What I thought was a well-planned biology literacy demonstration lesson soon turned into a nightmare. Little did I know that the text I brought wasn't going to meet any of the students' needs.

The hosting teacher and I had exchanged a flurry of emails. She asked that I introduce alleles as the kick-off to her genetics unit. At the time, I didn't even know what alleles were, but I had a few weeks to build my background knowledge on the topic, so I figured I could learn enough to fake it for a class period.

The teacher sent me the chapter questions from the textbook and graciously included the answer key. She rattled off a few objectives and made sure that I was clear that students had to know what alleles were because they would be asked to define them on the science department's common assessment.

The teacher reassured me that the class I would be working with was "lovely." She told me they were courteous, quiet, and very well behaved. She apologized that many of her students were struggling readers and that the textbook was too hard for them to read. For this reason, she suggested that I use science articles with the kids, as she did. Later that week, she emailed me several examples she had used with students so that I could gauge their reading level. The articles were engaging and had upper-elementary readability levels. Based on what she sent, I was confident that I could find science text about alleles that struggling readers could access.

I planned to model how to ask questions using a short text on cloning with the whole class. I would read a little and then think aloud questions I was wondering. I would read a little more and then paraphrase what I thought I understood. I would show students how to annotate in the margins and emphasize that they didn't need to write a lot—just enough to trigger their thinking. Students would then have a chance to try it on their own with the second half of the article. After students read, they would share out their thinking and then build their background knowledge by reading from the choice text options I had brought.

To prepare, I went to my favorite independent bookstore in Denver, The Bookies, and found several books about alleles, dominant and recessive genes, and Punnett squares. The books were written for younger readers but not insulting. With unfamiliar content, students would appreciate text below their grade level. The selections I purchased fit the bill . . . or so I thought.

Fast forward one week. I am armed with five different texts for students to choose from after I model my thinking. I grab the anchor text and begin my think aloud: "When I read science, I first look at the graphics. I don't start at the beginning of the page like I do with a novel. Next, I look to see if the graphic makes sense and if I have any questions about it."

I look around the room and everyone has their eyes on me, listening intently. Piece of cake, I think. I continue wondering aloud: "Why do some of the letters have a capital *B* and others have a little *b*?" Using the document camera, I write my question next to the Punnett square. I model my thinking in a few more places and then ask the kids to get up and select a text. No one moves. This is my first clue that something is wrong. At this point, their teacher quickly stands up and passes out the easiest text selection to everyone.

Students dutifully look down at the text, and for two minutes I watch what I initially think is reading. I notice that no one is annotating, so I decide to confer to find out why. Crossing the room, I spot a kid who has written the same thing on his text as I wrote on the screen. I kneel down next to him, and I can see Jorge neatly printed at the top of his page.

"Hi Jorge," I say. He looks up, and I can see a nervous smile. "I notice that you have the same question I had about this graphic. That's so weird. Are you thinking the same thing as I was?" Jorge holds his smile but doesn't say anything. Pointing to his question, I ask, "Are you really curious about this?" He looks at me and only shrugs his shoulders. "Here's the thing," I say, "your questions matter most. You don't have to wonder the same thing as I do. Let's try it together."

I ask Jorge to read the line aloud to see if he can decode. When he stays quiet, I assume that he is embarrassed to read aloud so I take the wheel. "OK, Jorge, no prob. I'll read aloud and then you can tell me what you are thinking." After reading a couple of lines, I pause. "So, what are you thinking?" He looks at me and then glances down at the text. The student next to Jorge whispers something to him in Spanish.

Quietly, Jorge responds, "Lo siento. No puedo leer esto en ingles."

Nervous now, because my Spanish is terrible and what I think I just heard was that he's sorry but he can't read in English. I ask, "Nada?"

He looks at me and shakes his head, while saying "Nada."

I smile at him and gently touch his arm. "Lo siento." I ask the student next to Jorge if he would please tell him that I'm sorry for not bringing text in Spanish. I quickly move across the room, and as I do, it becomes clear that most of the kids in the class can't read in English. Horrified, I realize that the text I have chosen won't work.

In a panic, I look to Sam for help. Normally she sits on the floor, close to kids so she can script conferences and small-group discussions. Her notes help teachers write more descriptive labels of what they see and hear in their debriefs. Her usual typing has stopped, which is never a good sign, and I notice she too is staring at me. "What do I do?" I ask.

With a chuckle and a shrug, she says, "I have no idea."

Embarrassed, I look to the group of teachers and apologize. "I'm not sure what to do next. The text I brought is too hard. I don't speak enough Spanish to know how to help them translate."

The class's teacher stands up and motions students to line up at the classroom door. Confused, the kids get up and head out of the room. Sheepishly, I give teachers a ten-minute break before we head into the debrief. As teachers start to gather, I wonder how to proceed. Everyone is quiet, and I begin the debrief by publicly apologizing to the hosting teacher. "I didn't realize they couldn't read English. When we talked about the students as readers, I must have misunderstood what you told me about their reading levels. Based on what we discussed, I thought that the text I brought would work. I'm sorry."

What happened next caught me off guard. The hosting teacher burst into tears and replied, "I didn't know you were going to have them read. I always read the science to them. I just assumed they understood because they are always so quiet." My heart went out to the hosting teacher. Obviously, it hadn't occurred to either of us to consider how many non-native English speakers were in the class. Lesson learned. Ask the hosting teacher how many English learners are in the class.

Listening comprehension and reading comprehension aren't the same beasts. And when kids are compliant, quiet, and polite, it doesn't mean they are engaged. It might just mean that they don't want to make waves. I still feel badly about that biology class, but the students taught me an important lesson—find out how many English learners are in the class and have choices of text for them. Had I known ahead of time, I could have had at least one choice of text in Spanish. I also could have brought in at least one piece of text that was an infographic. No matter what language a student speaks, they can still participate by reading and uncovering content from that text structure.

There is no hard-and-fast rule for "just right" text. It varies from student to student. The "just right" text in Spanish doesn't automatically translate to the "just right" text in English. A reading level that works in language arts may not work in science. No matter who or where I teach, I anticipate English learners in the class and make sure that the CYA structure of having text choices also includes something that non-native English speakers can access.

Tending to Text Selection

During the flurry of the school day, it can be easy to forget to put the needs of human beings before our urgency to cover content. When we take a little time to tend to what students might need to engage with and care about a text, we increase the number of teachers in the room—and students' opportunities to learn.

When we select texts that students might need or like, they are appreciative, especially the kid who wears the mask of the class clown. For this reason, I am constantly on the hunt for text that will hook each student. It's easier to do this when a unit is relevant and couched in a compelling topic. When this happens, I can usually find current events and informational text that meet students' needs. Sometimes, though, I have to tweak my case study to meet the needs of more students.

Midway through the first week, Vanessa hustles to her seat a little out of breath. "Miss Tovani," she puffs, "did you know we have refugees at our border?"

"I've been hearing a lot about kids from Mexico and Central America being taken away from their parents as they enter the US," I say, "but I'm not sure that makes them refugees. I wonder how a refugee is different from an undocumented immigrant? Maybe we need to investigate that."

Vanessa looks at me but doesn't say anything and then heads to her seat. I'm not sure if I shut her down or if she is thinking about what I said about being undocumented. I begin the minilesson for that part of the morning and then send kids off to work.

During work time, some students read informational texts about Syria, others work on their open letter, and a few return to their anchor text (*Refugee* by Alan Gratz or *Escape from Syria* by Samya Kullab). Vanessa motions me over to her table. I kneel down next to her and say, "What's up? Are you stuck?"

She shakes her head and asks, "Can I write my open letter about the border crisis? I'm sure people who are trying to come to the US are refugees. They are being forced to leave their homes just like people from Syria. I know people are leaving Mexico because of drug cartels. Families are scared."

"Well . . . ," I hesitate.

Vanessa doesn't wait for my answer, "My family made me leave Mexico. They knew I would be safer in the US and that if I stayed, I would be hurt by bad people. Parents have to get their kids out of Mexico to keep them safe."

I hear the urgency in her voice, and I start to coach myself. I tell the planned-out teacher side of me to be flexible. I worry that if I expand the option to read and write about the border crisis, I'll lose my focus. I'm torn because I can tell that this is a personal issue that Vanessa really cares about.

"OK, let's make a plan," I say. "Let me do a little research tonight on the border crisis. Let me see if there is enough text for you to research."

After school, I pick up Vanessa's folder to see what she's worked on for the day. I can tell she's read a lot of her anchor text by her completed inner voice sheet. I can also see that she started a beginning draft of her open letter. Prior to today, she hadn't written anything.

Traits of an Open Letter Written in First Person Point of View to a Public Figure or Organization but Intended for a Bigger Audience

- Identifies a serious issue in order to bring attention to it

- Encourages conversation about the serious issue

- Includes historical, scientific, and/or other factual content

- Shares a narrative to hook the reader

- Calls readers to take action

Dear,

* I want to write about this problem w/ the kids in the border but I do not nnow who to target, and don't nnow enough information about this case I would like to find new articles to read & get more informed.

Awesome! Thanks for letting me know. I found three different pieces of texts that you can read.

Figure 4.2
Vanessa's First Attempt (barf draft)

That night, I google "Child Separation at the Border," and more than enough text bubbles up. I begin to read. I learn that networks, newspaper, and social media are starting to take notice of the thousands of children being separated from their families and put in cages. The Trump administration's policy at the time is zero tolerance. I learn later that an asylee, like a refugee, flees violence and persecution. People seeking this status enter at points of asylum at United States borders. They turn themselves in. They aren't trying to sneak in, as some sources report. This peaceful surrendering is supposed to earn asylees a court hearing and protect them from the type of criminal prosecution that people crossing illegally might face. As families surrender, children are taken from their parents. The head of Homeland Security forcefully defends the policy, saying that the administration will not apologize for separating families. Her defense is, "We have to do our job. We will not apologize for doing our job. The Trump administration has a simple message— If you cross the border, we will prosecute you" (ABC News, June 18, 2018). Soon the administration faces a national outcry to reunite families. Unfortunately, it will be years later that we learn the full extent of this devastating policy.

That night, I decide I have to add this case study as an option. The next morning, I come to class armed with text. I have three articles that students can read to build their background knowledge about the crisis at the border. I also found two examples of opinion pieces on the issue that I can use as mentor texts for the writing that students are producing.

One is an open letter written by Laura Bush, the former first lady and wife of George W. Bush. The other, is from *USA Today* opinion page that shows an example of a short letter and two Facebook posts.

As class begins I say, "Yesterday, Vanessa asked if she could write about what's happening at the southern border. How many of you know what is going on down there?"

Arely raises her hand, and I'm shocked because this is the first time she has talked or even responded to me.

"What do you know about it, Arely?"

"Parents are just trying to save their kids."

I nod my head.

Thea, who is also quiet, responds, "It makes me angry. Parents are taking their children away from the crisis in Central America. They aren't the cause of the crisis. Why are parents getting punished?"

Luis, who also hasn't said much, jumps in: "The kids have no say when parents make the decision to leave Mexico. Why are the kids getting punished? Isn't being separated from their family going to be traumatic for them?"

Clearly, more students than Vanessa care about this issue. Several also seem to have a lot of background knowledge about it as well. "Thanks to Vanessa," I say, "I found two more examples of published writing that create awareness and call readers to action." I pass out Laura Bush's open letter and the opinion pieces from *USA Today*. I ask students to choose one to read and annotate. "As you read, notice what the author is doing and not doing. See if there is something that you might want to try in your writing."

Caleb grabs the shorter of the two. He starts to read the *USA Today* Facebook post. I see him writing, and then he blurts out, "I can do one as good as this."

"Probably better," I say. "What do you notice about the writing?"

"All this guy does is give his opinion. He doesn't even tell you why he thinks the way he does," says Caleb.

"True," I agree. "So as a reader, how does that make you feel?"

"I feel," Caleb says, smiling, "that the guy is an idiot."

I push back: "OK, probably not an idiot, but his writing isn't as strong as Laura Bush's or other examples we've read. Any guesses why?"

"Yeah, he doesn't have any facts or stories, or anything. He just tells you what he thinks. Who cares what this guy thinks?"

"And that Caleb, is why you want to have some evidence to support your opinion. If you can support your position, people will care more about what you think. But to do that, you may need to read some more about the southern border or Syria."

Caleb looks at me and says, "Where are the articles on Syria?"

Finding the right text for kids to read is important but so is finding the right text examples that show kids what you want them to create. Using examples of text that exist in the world mentors students and gives them a model to compare their work to. When kids wearing the mask of class clown see they are making something that actually exists in the world, the mask of silliness comes off. (In Chapter 5, you'll see more examples of how students use mentor texts to inform their writing.)

Up to this point, I had shown only one example of an open letter, and it was too sophisticated for a lot of the kids. It was an editorial titled "Why My State Won't Close Its Door to Syrian Refugees," by the governor of Washington State, Jay Inslee (*New York Times*, November 20, 2015). Even though I was just showing students what an op-ed/commentary looked like, many students like Caleb felt defeated when I introduced this example.

"You want me to write something like this?" he said. "Forget it. I can't write something that long or good."

At that point, Inslee's editorial was too sophisticated for Caleb to learn from and so, to avoid failure, he started fooling around. Caleb wasn't the only one who needed a less sophisticated example. Thanks to Vanessa's request to study the southern border crisis, I discovered two more opinion pieces that kids could use as models. Each one was more accessible than the other. Laura Bush's letter is beautifully written but less complex than Jay Inslee's. The *USA Today* opinion letter and Facebook post are poorly written with little sophistication. However, it was the Facebook post that Caleb could identify with. It was close to his current level of competency and served as an entry point for him to begin his writing.

When I tend to students' text needs and provide three different examples of the "big make," students breathe a sigh of relief and say, "Yeah, I can do this." They take the first step of writing, which is beginning a first draft. I try to find one example that is sophisticated, one that is little less sophisticated, and one that is not very good at all. This way, everyone in the class has a place to start from and, more importantly, a place to improve from.

Finding text that functions as an additional teacher in the room isn't hard to do if I am clear about why the topic matters. Some topics are trickier than others. Tending to text takes effort, but when students take off their masks of disengagement and get to work, it is well worth the time spent looking for the models. The three articles about the southern border hooked Arely, Luis, and Vanessa. The two additional opinion models hooked Caleb and gave him hope that he could produce something worth reading. I hook one kid and sometimes three at a time. That's how tending works.

Tending to Topics

When Vanessa asked if she could write her letter about the southern border crisis, I didn't have to throw out the whole unit as I originally feared. By tending to her concern, and letting her study a humanitarian crisis through a different lens, I was able to hook her and several others who were previously disengaged. This slight adjustment in the case study was more relevant to their lives than a place so far from home.

When kids vocalize that they don't care about a topic, teachers have a couple of ways to respond. One way is to blame them and hammer them for noncompliance. The other way is to figure out what they need in order to care. This requires a little empathy on the teacher's part. When I put myself in my students' shoes, I know that I learn from and work harder for someone who considers what I need to do my job well. When someone is trying to teach me something and they don't consider my needs, I sure don't want to take a risk in front of them and I definitely don't want to act like I care what they think.

On the other hand, when a teacher goes to the trouble of helping me understand why a topic is important and provides several ways for me to access information, I'm more willing to give the learning a go. When students ask, "Who cares about XYZ?" I want to be able to share compelling reasons why the learning matters and provide different texts that they can read to uncover content.

I take a lot of calculated risks in my teaching, and I am most vulnerable when I agree to do a demo in math or science (like the lesson on alleles!). I lack background knowledge in these disciplines, so I have to work harder to find relevance, context, and a purpose for knowing the information. Like some students, I often don't see a reason for learning about the topic, let alone teaching it. Let's head to another school where my demonstration lessons helped me understand the importance of being able to articulate why a unit of study matters.

Who Cares About the Rock Cycle?

While planning the demo, I asked the hosting teacher what she wanted kids to know about the rock cycle by end of the unit. She said, "The number one thing that students need to retain about the rock cycle is the process that rocks go through to become igneous, metamorphic, or sedimentary." She went on to warn me that kids usually don't get this because the process takes hundreds, even thousands of years to occur. "Most importantly," she continued, "the rock cycle is part of the curriculum, and there might be a question or two on the state test."

With all of the possible mask-wearers in mind, I search high and low for engaging and accessible text so that kids will have choice in what they read. I select strategies and carefully think through what I will model so that I am clear about what I want students to do. I barely sleep the night before, mulling over what kids will need in order to engage. I anticipate there will be students like me, who couldn't care less about the rock cycle. To save face, they might act out as a way to avoid looking stupid. To shore up my courage, I mistakenly remind myself that my job isn't to get kids to care about the rock cycle, but rather to help them comprehend science text so they do better on the state test. As you have might guessed, here comes another big fail.

Rodderick and the Rocks

Nervously standing in front of eighteen teachers, I watch the class of eighth graders stream into the room. As students enter, I ask them to notice the sets of rocks and minerals on their tables. I encourage them to pick up samples and examine each one. Students eagerly dive into the baskets. They forget about the visitors as they excitedly talk to each other about the treasure they hold.

After a bit, I ask students to pick up a blank notecard from the stack sitting next to the basket. I instruct them to jot down what they notice about their specimens.

The room quiets down. The students are now painfully aware of the eighteen teachers staring at them. They look to each other, not sure what to write. From the back of the room I hear a voice say, "They're just stupid rocks. What's the big deal?" Several students giggle. I look around to see who is wearing the class clown mask. Smirking as he balances his chair on two back legs, I see the tallest kid in the room.

Several teachers raise their eyebrows and look at me to see how I'll respond. "What's your name?" I ask.

With a southern twang he says, "Rodderick."

"Hey, Rodderick. Thank you for wondering the same thing I was."

Taken aback, he looks at me.

"Yeah, when I was asked to visit your room and teach you how to read scientific text better, I too wondered what was so great about the rock cycle." I wasn't bluffing. I'm thinking, *Seriously, what does the rock cycle have to do with the real world?* And if I remember correctly, the same thing is taught in second grade and then again in fifth grade. It's not like the majority of these eighth graders are going to be geologists. Few adults I know can rattle off the definition of igneous, metamorphic, or sedimentary rocks. Those who can, teach science, collect rocks, or are geologists.

Probably shocked that a teacher agreed with him, Rodderick is stunned into silence. For now. I plow ahead. Armed with decent text and a minilesson, I explain to students that I am going to show them how to keep their mind from wandering when they read something that is boring or hard.

Right on cue, Rodderick blurts out, "That's good because the stuff we read in here sucks."

Trying to get kids to pay attention to me and not Rodderick's floor show, I ignore his comment and say, "Watch what I do, because if you hate this kind of reading, it's going to help you remember what you read so you don't have to read it again."

Rodderick puts all four legs of the chair back on the floor and looks at the text reflected on the screen in the front of the class. I read a little of it out loud and then model how I am thinking about what I just read. I jot a few annotations on the text before going to the next few lines. I repeat the process two more times and then turn the reading, monitoring, and annotating over to students.

A few kids play along. Some take pity on me and others just rest their heads on their desks. I scurry from table to table, conferring with as many students as possible. I notice a few teachers whispering to each other and I think I overhear, "See, she can't teach these kids either."

I do a quick catch and pull the students together so I can model some more ways to annotate. But because I don't have a big reason to learn about the rock cycle, my annotations are too general. Having no reason to read other than "the material might be on the spring test" compounds students' disengagement.

Desperately, and maybe a little passive-aggressively, I model some questions about the topic that I genuinely have: Why is there so much oil in some states and not in others? Do oil deposits have something to do with the rock cycle? Are the Rocky Mountains shrinking? Is that because of erosion and is that part of the rock cycle?

After sharing several questions, I notice a few kids looking up. Rodderick has stopped cracking jokes to the kid next to him and gazes at the screen to see my questions. They aren't brilliant questions, but they are authentic and connect the isolated topic of memorizing types of rocks to the world outside of school.

Encouraged by the increased engagement and really wanting to know why the rock cycle matters, I continue modeling questions. "My niece wants to go to school in California, but I don't want her to go that far from home. I wonder if she knows there are earthquakes there? I wonder if earthquakes are part of the rock cycle? Maybe if I learn about earthquakes, I can scare her into not going to college so far away. How come some states have earthquakes and others don't? I've heard the Rocky Mountains are a result of earthquakes. I wonder if that's true?"

Looking around the room, I notice that I have most of the kids' attention. I stop asking my questions and challenge them to go back to their choice text to see if they can ask some questions that they care about. Heads bend down and kids get back on track.

Later that evening, I am at my hotel. I get out the students' work and start to read the annotations they have written. Almost everyone has a comment or question, even Rodderick. However, I can't tell if he is being silly or if his comment is genuine. He writes a connection: "When molten magma cools, it becomes an igneous rock. It must be hot because Taco Bell says its food is 'molten hot.'"

Zora wonders why rocks need names and then infers an answer with another question: "Is it so they can be sorted?"

Kaitlyn writes, "How does the rock cycle begin?"

Eva is surprised that there are rocks on the South Pole. George wants to know how minerals combine to make rocks and asks, "How come there are only three types of rocks compared to all the different kinds of minerals?"

Cynthia wants to know where to find rare and valuable rocks. Justice, who glared at the teachers all period, wrote, "Why are some rocks called pillow lava? That's a dumb name."

Natalie wants to know, "Are meteors rocks? And if they are, are they older than earth? How do you tell how old a rock is?"

Vincent writes, "How do rocks become land, and which rocks make crystals?"

Bria wants to know how rocks are shaped so that they can be used to make buildings and monuments. Cory wants to know what rocks have healing powers, while Jacob is curious to know how rocks become sand.

I'm actually surprised by their questions. Several connect to the revered "rock cycle," and contrary to their teacher's comments, students do seem to care. As I read through their questions, I discover misconceptions, what they think is interesting, and most importantly, what they want to know more about.

The next morning, I start the day off asking teachers to review their notes and share what they saw and heard. I can tell from their comments and questions that some teachers are impressed that I got Rodderick and some of the other "tough" kids to engage. I can also tell that some are unimpressed.

With great bravado, the science chair says, "It's great that Cris got Rodderick to behave, but she didn't teach the rock cycle. Kids have to know that because it could be on the test."

DeShawn, a math teacher, chimes in and wants to know why I didn't clear up all the misconceptions kids had.

Sarah, who teaches special education, is pleased that I addressed different reading levels with different pieces of text that students could choose from, but wonders how I find time to locate text. She says, "It's just so much easier and faster to use the textbook."

Jackie doesn't see the value of students' questions. She wants to know what students learned from their reading, not what they wondered. "If Cris had a worksheet with questions that kids could answer, we'd know if they learned anything." I refer Jackie to the list of student comments that I synthesized from their sticky notes. I ask her to read what kids wrote and challenge her to see if she notices any patterns about what students might know and need.

Donna must have missed the part where I modeled thinking, provided short text, and conferred with students, because she wants to know how I helped struggling readers.

Diana asks if I thought the rock cycle was important, because my questions gave students the impression that it wasn't. She goes on to say that she doesn't really think the rock cycle matters either but because it could be on the test, she has to cover it.

My demo that day sat in isolation. When one day doesn't connect to the next because the focus is on activities or isolated facts, students disengage, and teachers do too. It's hard to be stern with students like Rodderick who think topics are stupid when the only reason we give them is, "It might be on the test." That's not compelling, and it gives students who wear a mask of disengagement no reason to participate.

Fifty-Two Stories High

The view from the fifty-second floor of the "Cash Register Building" in downtown Denver is amazing. From that vantage point, I can see flat prairie lands to the east and the amazing Rocky Mountains to the west. I spot my neighborhood fifteen miles to the south and Mile High Stadium to the north. I see the sun setting in the west as the clouds gather to the south. It's a breathtaking view that provides a clear perspective of the entire Front Range. This high up, I notice the diverse topography of the land and the beauty of the Denver-Metro area. From this height, I can see in every direction, and it helps me get my bearings.

Thinking about long-term unit planning is a lot like viewing a city from the fifty-second story. It helps one see where they are and where they are going. It provides a roadmap to navigate roadblocks. Figuring out why a topic matters and is compelling is the first stop on the road to meeting the needs of all the mask-wearers in the classroom, but particularly the mask of the class clown. They need to know why something is worthy of more than five minutes of focus.

Not being a science teacher, I didn't have great responses to Rodderick's comments and questions. When he told me that rocks were stupid, I agreed. When he asked me what the big deal was about rocks, I shrugged my shoulders. Not only was I without a response, but so were the science teachers in the room. The only reason they gave for teaching the rock cycle was that there could be some questions on the test about it. If we don't know why the topic is compelling, we can't ask kids to think it matters, especially the class clowns who can make a joke out of anything. Fleshing out the need to know, before we get in front of students, matters.

Sometimes when I struggle to find out why a standard, topic, or unit of study is important, I use every available resource. For example, I go to search engines and type in, "Why does the rock cycle matter?" And I go to the Next Generation Science Standards and read what the series' authors think is important. And I google what geologists do. And, if I know people in the field, I ask them why kids and adults should know the information. I look for patterns—with connections to why the information and skills might have relevance and importance in the world outside of academia.

I was given no other reason to know the information other than memorizing the types of rocks for a possible test. Years later, after having to do this demo several more times, I dug into the topic and I realized that rocks and minerals impact people's lives every day! There are all kinds of compelling reasons to know about the topic.

While teaching Rodderick's class, I wasn't just missing a compelling reason for the study of the rock cycle. I was also missing several unit-based CYA structures. I didn't have any provocative questions. There was nothing to debate and no reason to read or write.

If I had had a "top-floor view" of this unit, I would have been able to tell students why the work they were doing mattered. The daily tasks would have had a greater purpose and meaning. During the demo, there was no real purpose to do the work, other than annotating random text for a stranger. There were no long-term or daily learning goals for kids to shoot for. At the time, I didn't know how useful learning targets were when it came to giving specific feedback and scaffolding students' learning. I didn't have any matched assessments for the unit, so students had to guess what I wanted. In hindsight, I should have planned with the teacher and used the standards as a tool to figure out what we wanted students to know and be able to do at the end of the unit. From there, I could have identified long-term targets that would have informed the daily makes.

I didn't have enough "top-floor" planning done to keep kids engaged. For example, in Rodderick's class, students wrote on sticky notes to demonstrate they could ask questions they cared about. Bam! They were done. They did the task. If I had done more long-term planning, those questions would have had a bigger purpose. Students' questions would then be a way for them to select text to build their background knowledge. It would also clue me into future texts that I should get into their hands. When students' questions are answered, their background knowledge and vocabulary grow, which then helps me get even MORE text into their hands. This cycle quickly dies, though, if students don't know why they are building background knowledge.

Without a purpose and audience for students to share their thinking, the work becomes drudgery. If I can put the learning in context by connecting it to what professionals in the world make and do, students are more apt to stay engaged. When I know what students will create at the end of the unit to demonstrate that they've hit the standards, the daily targets and makes have more relevance.

If I had a chance to do Rodderick's demo over, I'd plan an assessment with the teacher that would give students a chance to demonstrate they've hit the standards. Maybe students could have written a recommendation to a city planner, explaining why certain areas should or shouldn't be developed based on topography. This is something that a geologist might do. In the proposal, students would have to explain the science in a clear and intelligible way—and use a model to show why certain areas are good or not so good to develop. Heads up, though: if you just *pretend* that the letters are going to a city planner and you don't actually send them, students will soon lose the urgency that an authentic audience provides.

"What about a chapter test?" you might ask. Sure, a chapter test is a way to assess knowledge, but in order to show that they really understand the big ideas, students need to apply that knowledge using the behaviors and habits that scientists use in the world. An objective test might show that they've temporarily memorized facts, but that doesn't mean they can think like a scientist.

Today, when I am doing even a one-day demonstration lesson, I create a long-term plan and think about possible long-term ways for students to show their understanding of the unit's standards at the end. These big makes, or summative assessments, help me figure out what students need daily.

When students decide that a topic isn't worthy of their time, they act out to combat boredom. When teachers take time to flesh out compelling reasons for students to care about a complex topic, using provocative questions and connections to local issues, students have more reasons to invest their efforts and fewer reasons to be the class comedian.

What Makes a Topic Compelling?

Unlike teaching facts in isolation, juicy topics serve as Velcro that binds the content to memory so students can construct meaning. Compelling topics grab class clowns by the heart and dare them to care.

Topics that compel me to learn have several features in common. They are timeless and connected to a current event or issue. I am curious about why something is occurring or has happened. There is an aspect of controversy connected to the issue that forces me to explore different perspectives. These perspectives lead me to stories that have powerful narratives driving my need to know. In other words, I want to study topics that are worthy of my time. I want this for students as well.

I know that I've found a compelling topic when I can connect it to an interesting case study or gripping current issue. Linking the topic to a case study and/or a captivating current issue makes it possible for students to remember what they've learned and apply their new learning to different topics, time periods, and issues. When I find a compelling topic, it facilitates my long-term planning because I can return to the topic year after year, refreshing it by linking it to a current event or case study.

If you are locked into teaching a specific novel or topic, don't despair. When I am asked to "teach" a particular work of literature, I reframe the directive by examining why the text is so compelling. I ask myself, "Of all the books kids could read, why is someone mandating this one?" A lot of my English teacher friends believe that literature is a reflection of the human experience. If I were a math teacher, I'd probably roll my eyes at this. But if I identify themes in literature, I often see similar struggles that people face today.

When I was told that eleventh-grade had to read *The Great Gatsby* (Fitzgerald 1925), I folded the themes into a study about the dark side of the American dream. We examined how far Americans would go to get what they want. We argued about whether the American dream is still possible for students today. We questioned its attainability and debated whether everyone has an equal chance to achieve it.

When I was told to "teach" *Catcher in the Rye* (Salinger 1951), we exploded the themes of adolescent angst by exploring issues like lying, procrastination, and feelings of inadequacy. Students compared their avoidance behaviors to Holden's and recognized if not themselves, then other teens who faced feelings similar to those that Holden did. We read about defense mechanisms and how people use them to avoid suffering. Students examined their own motivations and wrote about healthier ways to face adversity.

Using *The Things They Carried* (O'Brien 1990) as an anchor text helped us to explore war and its effects on individuals and society. We studied post-traumatic stress disorder and the problems that many veterans face when they return home, like homelessness, mental health challenges, and poor healthcare.

If there isn't an assigned piece of literature to build my compelling topic around, I start with a topic and then look for the text. For example, the problem of war and how it affects individuals and society is timeless. It will always be part of human existence. When there isn't a clear text or a topic to choose from, I look to timely current events or issues. For example, the horrific separation of children from their parents at the United States southern border is happening as I write this, in 2020. When this atrocity ends, and the current crisis is over, the issue of unjust internment will still be a compelling topic. Sadly, somewhere in the world, it will still be happening.

I Don't Want to Get Political

"I have to be very careful about my political views around here," a teacher says to me, "I can't bring controversy into my classroom."

"Why?" I ask.

"Lots of parents support what X, Y, and Z are doing in the White House, and I don't want to rock the boat."

For whatever it's worth, here's my take on this issue. Our job as teachers is not to convince students to believe what we believe. Part of our job is to teach them how to take a position and defend it with solid evidence. It's not about indoctrinating students. It's about helping them research, analyze, and synthesize ideas so that they can discover who they are and what they want their world to be. In the classroom, it doesn't matter what I think the United States should do about anything. What matters is that I can show students how to argue their thinking in a polite and logical manner.

When we welcome all student perspectives, our job description shifts from indoctrination to instruction. This allows us to focus on teaching students how to read, research, and write arguments that are defensible. It's not about all of us agreeing. It's about studying an issue, examining it from multiple perspectives and then providing evidence to support the position that we choose to take.

I understand the need to keep ourselves safe as teachers. The last thing any of us wants to do is spend hours trying to repair relationships with parents who think we are trying to brainwash their children. When I have my reasons at the ready, I can share them with anyone who may worry that I'm supporting terrorism by studying the Syrian refugee crisis. Below are some of my compelling reasons:

Compelling Reasons to *Read and Write* About a Humanitarian Crisis Case Study: The Syrian Refugee Crisis

- The behaviors and mindsets we choose affect our actions.

- Stories help us see different perspectives, which can give us empathy, understanding, and a roadmap for how we might act in a particular situation.

- Taking a position on a controversial issue is scary. Supporting that position with evidence makes it less scary and my argument more credible. Doing this is difficult if I, as a learner, don't know about the topic. Writers need to read and build their background knowledge before they can write well about an issue.

- Knowing how to read and write complex text empowers learners to be successful not only in school but in life.

- Sharing stories of human resettlement creates counter narratives necessary to fight social injustice. Knowing the stories of different cultures, people, and situations helps us to push back against stereotypes and day-to-day discrimination. Stories can teach and help us to be more empathetic.

Compelling Reasons to *Study* a Humanitarian Crisis:
Case Study: The Syrian Refugee Crisis

- When violence erupts or a catastrophic weather event happens, life can change in a matter of minutes, shattering families and communities and driving millions to flee. Everyone is vulnerable.

- Crises, whether human-made or natural, cause immense suffering and uncertainty, not only because victims lose loved ones, homes, and livelihoods, but because their safety net also disappears.

- Some governments try to guarantee the security and human rights of their citizens, but they are often unable to do so, and sometimes they become violators. The tragic result is that displaced civilians are extremely vulnerable to targeted violence, sexual assault, exploitation, persecution, and other human rights abuses.

- Being able to describe the social, economic, and political impact of world crises helps people make decisions. It impacts how they respond, vote, treat others, and spend money.

- Being able to weigh the risk of ignoring crises helps us to think about: How does ignorance play into fear? Who should we stand up for? Who would help me if I were struggling? How do I distinguish what is propaganda, authentic news, or a bald-faced lie?

Why Controversy Matters

I carefully read standard one from the eleventh- and twelfth-grade Common Core English Language Arts Writing Standards and realize that I don't know how I can teach students to hit this standard if I never give them a chance to argue:

> CCSS.ELA-Literacy.W.11-12.1 Write arguments to support claims in an analysis of substantive topics or texts, using valid reasoning and relevant and sufficient evidence.

Students need opportunities to wrestle with controversy. If there is only one right answer, it's hard to construct an argument.

I know that I've landed on a compelling topic when it is surrounded by controversy. Studying a humanitarian crisis, such as the one Syria is embroiled in, is controversial. There are hotly contested political views because there are humanitarian, national security, and economic development issues connected to the topic. This complexity is necessary because it gives students a chance to examine differing points of view and engage in critical thinking. Engaging in critical thinking helps students make choices about what they value and how they will take action or ignore the situation.

All kids deserve a chance to argue and to know how to do it well. When I value compliance over controversy, I'm just asking for students to disengage. After a while, vanilla gets boring. Students who wear the mask of the class clown thrive on controversy. They want to argue. They need to argue. They are tired of being told to memorize and spit back information. Learning reasons why they feel a certain way about an issue and then being able to articulate those reasons is empowering—and gives them the stage they clamor for.

The View from the Street

Checking out the city from the street below the fifty-second floor of the "Cash Register Building" provides a completely different perspective of the city. Horns honk, jolting drivers out of their daze. Bike couriers whiz past cars stopped at lights. Pedestrians move in waves to their scheduled destinations. It's sometimes hard to get your bearings from the street level. Tall buildings block the view of the mountains so I don't know what direction is west. If I don't pay attention to what is right in front of me, I could stumble or lose my way. While the view from the fifty-second floor helps me to see the big picture of the city, the street-level view is up close and personal. I can't see the big picture from here, but this is where all the action is.

I like to think of planning in terms of views. When I plan a unit from the fifty-second floor, I'm looking at the big picture of what students will do over a six-to-eight-week unit. When I plan for the street-level view, I'm thinking about the day-to-day work that students will do. Lately, in coaching and planning sessions, I've started to ask teachers what their bottom line is. I ask, "If you could structure class so that students could only do a few things each day, what would they be?" When teachers know their bottom lines, it's easier to protect instructional time from daily distractions that leach precious minutes.

I keep this idea in my head when planning units. I ask myself constantly, *What will keep students reading, writing, and discussing longer?* Thinking about my bottom line helps me to sift and sort what matters most. When I planned the unit around the Syrian refugee crisis, I decided on four areas of focus for students:

1. **Learn more about the world outside of the students' neighborhood.**
Many students will be eligible to vote in the next presidential election. Knowing more about global issues will give them some background knowledge when they hear candidates, bosses, friends, and family speak about where they stand on current hot topics.

2. **Argue politely and logically with someone who has a different point of view.**
I want students to understand that complex issues can be viewed from multiple perspectives and when we learn about differing perspectives, it gives us insight. Talking to others in a respectful way helps us develop our position on issues. The ability to have discussions with people who see the world differently is an important life skill. Being able to do this will empower students for the rest of their lives as they collaborate with colleagues and peers to find solutions to important problems.

3. **Increase students' reading and writing endurance and proficiency.**
The first day of class I notice that many students quit at the first sign of difficulty. Caleb isn't the only one who avoided work in the beginning. It's true for all learners; when they don't know what else to do, they quit. This means they have to learn to negotiate different kinds of complex text. They have to acknowledge that complicated issues often have more than one right answer. And the hardest truth of all is that clearly conveying thinking in the written form, is hard. Good writing rarely happens on a first draft. Writers have to revise!

4. Grow students' sense of themselves as learners.

I want students to see that it's not too late for them to become good readers and writers. I want to switch their mindset from *I can't do this because I'm a bad reader and writer* to *I can do this because I know that when learning gets challenging, I'm getting smarter.* When students see themselves as learners, they keep going when the going gets tough.

The daily structure that helps me ensure that students get the bulk of time to read, write, and discuss is the workshop model structure. Workshop model helps me chunk and use time to plan how and what students will read, write, and discuss. On a daily basis, I want students to grow their thinking, their background knowledge, and their ability to read and write. When I've viewed the unit from the fifty-second floor and done some long-term planning, the day-to-day planning isn't as grueling. Planning with workshop model in mind helps me navigate learning at the street level.

To maximize students growth, my goal is to get them working two-thirds of the class minutes, which only leaves me one-third of the time to model, lecture, or demonstrate something new to the whole class. Workshop model helps me structure time so that students are practicing the skills they need to be more skillful readers, writers, thinkers, and problem solvers. Instead of passively listening, I want them reading a variety of text structures, writing to grow and demonstrate understanding, and talking to articulate their thinking.

As a reminder, here are the components of the workshop model that I use to ensure student learning:

> **The Opening:** The opening sets the purpose for the day and clarifies why the learning matters. It gives students a vision for work time by reviewing the learning targets and the daily "makes and do's." By providing a variety of thinksheets and tasks, I can help students decide how they will hold and show their thinking. Students ask themselves, *How will I hold my thinking today so I can use it later to communicate my understanding when I create an authentic product?*
>
> For the class clown, the opening helps them envision how their time will be spent getting smarter and connecting with others, instead of plotting when they will lob the next snarky comment to entertain themselves and others.

Work Time for Students: Work time is an opportunity for students to practice their learning and create new thinking. Maybe not new thinking for the world, but new thinking for themselves. During work time, students have autonomy to decide what they will read and write. This means that I have a variety of texts that students can choose to read and a variety of ways that they can re-enter their writing.

During this time, class clowns can rework, revise, and build their reading and writing endurance. When students generate work, it gives me an opportunity to give them feedback. I can do this in a conference or by writing a few comments on their thinksheets or drafts. This feedback holds the class clown accountable on a daily basis. Knowing that they will have time each day to return to their work gives them a chance to experiment and build their skill set. It can also energize them because it's a chance for the teacher to give input so that they can be more productive the following day.

Work Time for Teachers: While the students are reading, writing, and talking to grow their knowledge and skills, I have two main roles: get to know individuals better through conferring and manage the sequence of tasks and time.

For me, conferring is the heart of the workshop model and where I do most of my teaching. It's a place where I can give individuals personal attention. I can listen to students and guide their learning. It's also a way to hold them accountable, not in a punitive way, but in a way that says, "Your thinking matters and I want to know more about it." Conferring with class clowns gives them the stage and an audience of one versus the whole class! When I confer, I notice patterns in the work students leave me. This helps me plan my minilesson and an ideal sequence of tasks for the next day.

My other role during work time is to manage time. For example, I anticipated that students could read for twelve minutes before I would need to do a catch. But when I looked up from a conference, fourteen minutes had passed, so I let students keep going. Other times, the room explodes at nine minutes of reading. This means I need to do a catch to figure out what kids need. Catches are opportunities for the teacher to adjust the task, text, or target. It's also an opportunity to redirect, reteach, and review what it is we want students to do to help them return to the work of reading, writing, and discussing. Short catches rarely last longer than a minute. They break up the work time and can be a gift to the class clown, who might need ideas for what to work on next.

Minilesson/Model: The minilesson is the opportunity for teachers to build background knowledge, model thinking, or demonstrate how to do something. Sometimes, I model how I tackle a complex text. Other times, I show a film clip to provoke thinking or to create curiosity for a topic. I might model a revision strategy or a way to get unstuck. During this portion of workshop, I can give students information on how to use work time minutes to grow their thinking. I can do this by showing student writing or thinking examples from the previous day's work time. Kids who wear the mask of the class clown love when their thinking is highlighted. They relish the attention and they will then work with more focus to get their thinking publicly highlighted again.

Debrief: The debrief is a quick way for students to reflect on the targets or their learning for the day. When I'm too busy to look at lots of student work, the thinking that students leave me during the debrief can often give me insight into what individuals or the whole class might need for the next day. For the class clown, the debrief gives them a chance to honestly articulate what they learned and need next.

The components of workshop model provide opportunities for me to plan ways to spur and focus reading, writing, talking, and thinking. It also gives me a chance to give students who crave attention, just enough of it to keep them from demanding it from the entire room.

My golden rule is that every day, I want to make sure we are all clear on the purpose for the learning—and this includes me! I want to model a reading, writing, or talking behavior so that students can practice the skills that will help them deepen understanding. If students are going to become better readers, writers, and thinkers, they need the bulk of workshop time to practice and reflect on these behaviors. Here's what workshop as a structure and sequence of task and time might look like in practice . . .

It's afternoon and the kids have gone home. I am quickly looking through students' exit tickets from earlier in the day. I read Caleb's: "Who is this Bashar guy and why is he bombing his own people?" Getting online, I easily find an informational piece about Syria's current leader. I put the text in his work folder so I don't forget to give it to him tomorrow morning. I make a few extra copies in case other students want to know more about the ruthless dictator. Caleb's question serves as an output that helps me know what to input the next day.

The following morning, after a short minilesson, I look around the room to see who I will confer with first. I know for sure that at some point during the period I have to confer with Caleb to get him writing more. But for now, he is quietly reading the informational piece about Syria's president Bashar al-Assad. By inputting the article, I will hopefully stimulate some output in his writing. While I have a chance, I head over to quiet Thea to see how she is doing. After about seven minutes, noise starts to erupt at Caleb's table. I finish my conference with Thea and stand up to monitor the room. I scan it to notice what kids need next. Is it time for a catch? Or is one person blowing up the work time?

I can tell it's time for a catch. "Time out, you guys. Eyes up here." Students look my way. "It seems that people are getting stuck. What do you need to get back into your work?" No one says anything at first.

Then, right on cue, Caleb breaks the silence: "I need a break." A few kids laugh, and the girls at the front table roll their eyes. I ask students to look at the clock and remind them that our reading and writing endurance goal for the day is twenty-five minutes. We are only at twelve. I mentally pause the work time clock. I ask kids to go back to their reading and writing to find a question or something that they learned to share with their tablemates. They need time to talk before returning to the reading and writing.

At their tables, students start to share by reading aloud from their annotations and double-entry diaries. Some piggyback their thinking off the original sharer's comments, while others still aren't sure how to do that.

After four or so minutes of talk time, I catch students again. "OK, we're going back into the work time." Then I share a few things they can do if they are tired of what they were doing during the first twelve minutes. I tell students:

- You can choose another article to read to build more background knowledge.

- You can read from your anchor text novel or your free-choice book.

- You can work on your double-entry diary or work on your current draft of the open letter.

- You can also grab a firsthand account from one of the refugee stories. This might help you hit the learning target of embedding narrative.

Then I ask Caleb, "What are you going to do next?"

"After I go to the bathroom, I'm going to come back to my seat and write about this Bashar guy. People need to know what he is doing."

"Great, hurry up in the bathroom. I'm timing you." I don't really time him but I want him to know that I expect him to move fast. Caleb needs movement. Keeping him from going to the bathroom will only prolong his off-task behavior, which will also bother other students. I ask a few more people to share aloud what they are going to work on next as a model for the ones who aren't sure what to do. As kids get back to work, I resume my conferring.

When I plan my daily lessons using workshop model as a structure, more kids get to be engaged for more minutes of the class period. In the olden days, I used to think about what I was going to do—not what the kids were going to do. Often this meant I was killing myself doing all the work. When this happens, it's an open invitation for the class clown to steal the show.

These daily lesson structures help me stay true to the maxim Samantha Bennett writes about in *That Workshop Book: New Systems and Structures for the Classrooms That Read, Write, and Think* (2007), whoever is doing the reading, writing, and talking is the one doing the learning. When class clowns are engaged—behaviorally, emotionally, and cognitively—they put their wits to good use talking back to the text and to their classmates about topics and ideas that matter.

If I want students to work for two-thirds of the time, I can't just say, "Go work!" I've got to give students reasons to stay engaged. This is where the CYA structures and long-term planning come into play. They provide different reasons for students to stay engaged longer.

Once I've figured out the big ideas and reasons for students to read, write, and talk, I can begin to envision how the days will roll out over time. This is the street-level view that connects the day-to-day work to the bigger learning goals.

What Works? Five CYA Strategies That Help Students Put Away Their Class Clown Mask:

1. Do your own research to figure out why your **Topic** matters. Try to connect what you believe is "key" to what professionals who need the information actually do. Consider how the work students will do aligns to what professional in the field do. Then connect it to what the standards say. When you can articulate why the topic matters and find different and interesting ways for students to uncover content, the class clown mask-wearers are less likely to try to steal the show.

2. Authentically model how you might get started with the **Tasks** you want students to attempt. Model how to ask authentic questions that you care about. Show students how they can use those questions to drive engagement. Model how to make meaning and negotiate difficulty with boring or difficult text.

3. **Tend to** student comments seriously and answer with honesty and vulnerability. For example, "Yeah, when I was asked to visit your room and teach you how to read scientific texts better, I too wondered what was so great about the rock cycle."

4. Don't shy away from controversial issues. They give students **Targets** that will encourage them to examine differing points of view and engage in critical thinking. Engaging in this kind of critical thinking helps students make choices about what they value and how they will take action.

5. Strive to structure every class period with two-thirds of the **Time** for students to practice reading, writing, and discussing. As the teacher, work to learn about each student's background knowledge, skills, and interests so you can get more **Text** into their hands. When you are clear on your role as "chief listener" in the room, the class clown mask-wearer won't need to distract attention away from the work of getting smarter.

Chapter 5

The Mask of Minimal Effort

*Kids are not the future. They are the present, and they
need to do work now that matters.*

—*Yesenia, seventh grader, 2018 National Conference
EL Education: Educating for a Better World*

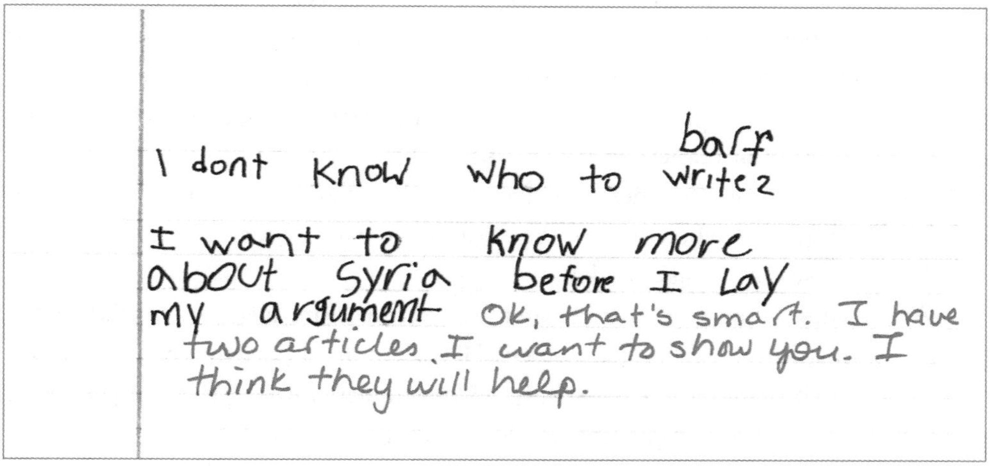

I dont know who to barf write2

I want to know more
about Syria before I lay
my argument Ok, that's smart. I have
two articles. I want to show you. I
think they will help.

Figure 5.1
Johnny's Barf Draft

Despite what it says in the upper right-hand corner of Figure 5.1, the name of the student who produced this work sample is not "barf." It's Johnny, which he incidentally did not put on his paper. However, he did correctly label his first draft of writing as his *barf draft*. It is the third day of class. In an attempt to assess what students know and think about the Syrian refugee crisis, I ask them to write to one of the provocative questions. To alleviate some anxiety that "on-demand" writing can create, I say to students, "Pick a question that interests you and just barf out whatever thinking you have about it."

- Is the United States losing its humanity? Why?

- How do I decide when to take action, and if I choose to, what can I do?

- Should the United States resettle its "fair share" of refugees? Why?

- Is everything destined to be, or can I change my fate? Why?

This first-draft thinking will eventually morph into an open letter that students will send to an audience of their choice. I have multiple learning goals for students as they write their open letter. First, so their writing improves, I want students to do more than one draft. Second, I want their letter to be of high quality so they will be confident to send it to an audience bigger than me. Writing for someone other than their teacher gives students more urgency to produce quality work. Last, I want students to build background knowledge about the Syrian refugee crisis so they understand it well enough to take a position on the issue, support it with evidence, and then call on their readers to take action.

I explain to the class that their final demonstration of understanding will take place eight weeks from now when we host the Awareness, Empathy, and Action Summit.

"What's a summit?" asks Caleb.

"A summit is when great thinkers get together to create awareness, build empathy, and brainstorm solutions to a problem." I explain that I have invited community members who have experience working with refugees. During the summit, each visitor will join a table group of five students and listen to their thinking about the crisis. Our guests will have a chance to share knowledge and their perspectives concerning the relocation of displaced people. I also explain to students that they will be the ones carrying the conversation. Having adults who have worked in the field share their perspectives will also help students integrate new thinking. This summit will give students an opportunity to demonstrate that they have hit several long-term learning targets:

Long-Term Learning Targets

- I can use thinking strategies to read, write, and discuss complex issues.

- I can logically and politely articulate my position and support it with evidence.

- I can describe the effects of a humanitarian crisis on individuals and society.

"Are we really going to have people come in and talk to us?" asks Caleb.

"Yes," I say. "But they aren't talking TO you. You are going to have a conversation WITH them. And it's going to be pretty awkward if you don't have anything to say."

With a bit of panic in his voice, Caleb responds, "I don't even know what to write, let alone say."

"Well, you've got eight weeks to get smarter about it. As you revise your open letter you will get clearer and clearer on what you want to say and ask at the summit."

"Who am I gonna write this stupid letter to, anyway?" Caleb sulks.

"I don't know," I say. "That's up to you. I'm writing mine to the director of homeland security."

"Who's that?"

"It's the person who works at the national level in our government to make sure our cities and towns are safe. This department deals with domestic emergencies, like terrorism. It is also in charge of immigration."

Suspiciously, Caleb asks, "We're seriously gonna send these letters to people?"

"Yeah," I say. "Our job is to create awareness for others about this serious problem and decide if and how we might help or relocate refugees. There's no use in doing all this research and learning if no one else is going to see your thinking." I stop talking to see if Caleb is buying it.

> **Possible Audiences for Student Writing**
> - President
> - First lady
> - Facebook page
> - Director of homeland security
> - Local paper
> - School paper
> - Instagram
> - Family member
> - Local government officials

It's evident from students' barf drafts that they are not ready to take a position. Many admit they know nothing about the topic. Additionally, they have no idea to whom they should write. This might be the first time it has occurred to them that school writing could be for an audience bigger than their teacher.

Eight weeks will go fast. That's only forty hours of instruction. Barring active shooter drills, student announcements, and all the other interruptions that teachers endure, students only have 2,400 minutes to get ready for the Awareness, Empathy, and Action Summit. Based on everyone's first attempt, we will need every minute to read, write, and research this important issue.

If Only I Could Read My Teacher's Mind

I understand kids who wear the mask of minimal effort. Many times, they put the mask on because they are scared! In classes when I felt like I had to divine what the teacher wanted, I grew hopeless. I vividly remember sitting in the library my freshman year of college trying to figure out how to write a literary analysis. I was angry at myself for not learning how to do it in high school. I felt lonely, incorrectly assuming that I was the only one who didn't know how to write in ways the professor required. I started multiple drafts, wishing I could read his mind. After hours of struggling, I didn't know what else to do, so I wrote a short, rambling, one-and-done draft that was a bunch of garbage. When I received the paper back there were minimal comments like *awk, frag, what?* and then a C- at the bottom of the last page.

I had no idea how to do the *next* writing assignment any better, so I complied, and wrote another short, rambling, one-and-done draft. I'm not sure if my professor thought I was lazy based on what he read, but what I do know is that my writing didn't get better.

Thirty-five years later, I can now articulate what I needed most from my professor. In my experience, students who wear the mask of minimal effort need the following supports:

- A model or mentor text to see what strong and weak products look like.

- An authentic purpose and an audience with whom to share the work. Going public increases urgency to revise.

- Clear criteria for success with learning targets connected to a model.

- More than one learning target to choose from when revising.

- Opportunities to get feedback in between drafts and before the final draft is due. Feedback too late is useless!

Many students want to please teachers and do what is asked of them. In order to satisfy my professor, I needed more than a description of the assignment. I needed to know the *how* of actually doing it. When the *how* is never shown, learners cheat, give up trying, and do whatever it takes to keep safe. To do that, they wear the mask of minimal effort.

In order to show they have hit the standards I am going for, students will have to do more than write a paper or take a test. They need something more complex to show their understanding. I don't want students to have to try to read my mind of what I want them to know and be able to do. So, I sketch out a rough plan starting with the performance task that they will do at the end. In this case it is the Awareness, Empathy, and Action Summit. In order for students to demonstrate that they can politely and logically discuss the Syrian refugee crisis with community members, they will need:

1. **Real guests and deadlines.** I recruit knowledgeable, adult participants from a variety of government and nongovernment support agencies. I want to make sure that there are diverse panelists and perspectives represented. It is important for students to see themselves and others represented in the guests I invite. Sometimes, I just put out a call on Facebook and I find lots of leads. I also contact churches, local universities, and nonprofits to see how they can help. I make a concerted effort to make sure that the panel doesn't just represent whiteness. I send the invitees a date and time so they can RSVP and add the event to their busy calendars. An authentic deadline replicates due dates in the world, and both the students and I have a goal. This helps me prioritize how we spend our daily work time so students can build their background knowledge and skills and be ready to have a discussion with a knowledgeable person about the Syrian refugee crisis.

2. **Lots of nonfiction to read.** Sometimes we ask students to write too soon. As Johnny wrote in his barf draft, he needed more information before he could "lay his argument." Reading lots of nonfiction helps students to view an issue from multiple perspectives so they can take a position.

3. **Narratives and firsthand accounts to read.** This text structure gives students a sense of the trials and tribulations of people who are displaced. Embedding a short narrative in the open letter they write will also help readers care about their argument.

4. **A well-written open letter.** Students will feel confident to intelligently discuss the issue after they have written an argument that clearly outlines their position and is accompanied by supporting evidence.

5. **An authentic audience.** When students write for people who don't know and love them like their teacher, there is a greater urgency to revise. Clear learning targets help students know how to improve their drafts, because their teacher can use the targets to give specific feedback.

6. **Models.** Starting with my initial drafts, I show students weak and strong models of the product they are creating. When students see that I value the assignment enough to do it myself, they view the task as being worthy of their time. I demonstrate that I too am a writer, not just an "assigner," and because I am going through the same process as they are, I can help them negotiate difficulty.

Sketching out a quick planning model of my unit helps me add multiple inter-connected layers of reasons for students to read, write, and talk.

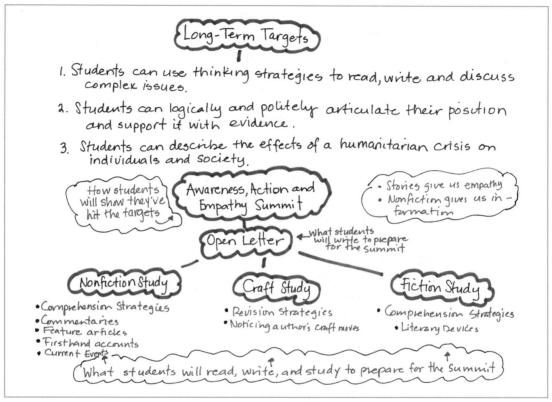

Figure 5.2
Syrian Refugee Crisis Unit Sketch

Showing What Success Looks Like by Analyzing a Model

When I was a kid, I played competitive tennis. We didn't have a lot of money for private lessons so my dad tried to help me the best he could. He was a good athlete and a decent tennis player, but sometimes I had trouble doing what he modeled. I am a lefty and he was a righty. Like most lefties, I got good at watching other people do things as mirror images. Most of the time, I could observe my dad and then use what I saw to improve a skill. But when it came to improving my serve, I couldn't translate his opposite arm and leg movements to mine. Dad knew that I needed a better model than he could provide. So, every chance we got, we'd watch televised matches of the then greatest lefty of all time—John McEnroe.

My dad focused my observations. He'd say, "Watch his left foot. Notice how it stays planted until the racket hits the ball. Do you see how he keeps his right arm straight as he tosses the ball in the air? Pay attention to the head of the racket and the point where it makes contact with the ball." Dad labeled what success looked like. He didn't just say, "Serve like McEnroe." He identified the criteria: front foot planted, straight arm toss, racket contacts the ball before it starts to drop. His articulation of what a great server did gave me clear goals when practicing my own serve. It also gave him a way to target his feedback after he watched me play a match.

"You did a good job tossing the ball today. You kept your arm nice and straight. Remember when you struggled to get your serve in during the second set? Your front foot was bouncing around. You foot-faulted three times. You're lucky you didn't get called on that. By the third set, you kept that foot planted. Were you aware that you made that change?"

Even though my dad built fences for a living, he was a great teacher. Without even knowing it, he was teaching me to be metacognitive. He wanted me to be able to recognize the qualities of a good serve so that I could not only practice it, but also correct it when things started to get off track.

I think about the students I teach now and how important it is to not only model for them, but also to give them opportunities to practice and own the skill, so it can be applied and readjusted to meet the needs of new situations. Johnny and the rest of the class not only needed to know what a high-quality open letter looked like; they also needed to know the components that made that genre unique.

It's interesting to watch which masks appear when students aren't sure that they can do what is being asked of them. When I introduced the open letter assignment, I could see Johnny shutting down. Caleb started acting out. The leap was too big for both of them. Both readily admitted that they didn't know what an open letter was, why someone would write one, or how to even begin. So instead of giving it a try, they pushed back with off-task behavior. Their goal was not only to avoid reading and writing; if Caleb could distract others and Johnny could slip through the cracks, it would serve as a way to take the focus off of the task.

Devon, on the other hand, who was a frequent wearer of the mask of minimal effort, tried another tactic. On the back of another handout, he confidently wrote his first, second, and final drafts of the open letter. Ha! Little did he know he was far from being finished.

Before the bell rang, he handed me his paper, and as he headed back to his seat, Caleb asked, "Are you done?"

"Dude," Devon said, "it's not that hard. Just answer the question."

Authentic Artifacts and Mentors: Meet the Guest Teacher

After reading students' first attempts to write their open letter, I can see that they need more background knowledge and some models of what I want them to write. The following class period, students read the board where the following learning targets are posted:

- I can ask questions I am curious about.

- I can ask questions about parts I don't understand.

- I can use a mentor text to inform my writing.

As the year progresses, students get into the habit of reflecting on the targets and sharing any questions they have about them during the opening minutes of class. The next step is for them to identify what they will do during work time to meet the targets. (For more examples of learning targets see Appendix A.)

I pass out a clean copy of the op-ed I described in Chapter 4. Op-eds have many similarities to open letters. I return to the one written by Jay Inslee, the governor of Washington State, who wrote an editorial on the Syrian refugee crisis. When I find a well-written example of text, I can use it more than once with students. Sometimes I use the example as a model to study other writers' craft moves. I can also use the piece to help students build their background knowledge as they practice a reading strategy. For today, the minilesson plan is to show how I annotated the first page, but I only think aloud for the first few paragraphs. Then I hand it over to students so they can practice listening to their inner voices. I make time for students to read the piece once to clarify questions and to get a gist of the argument. On the second read, students will use the learning target rubric to compare what the governor wrote to the listed learning target criteria. This can take up to two class periods depending on how long the class period is.

Press releases are official statements issued to news organizations giving information on a specific issue. What is the issue?

Press Release

November, 2015

(Obama was president when this was written.)

ISIS

Over the last week, a growing number of governors, representatives, senators and presidential candidates have demanded that America slam shut our borders to refugees who are fleeing unspeakable horrors at the hands of the Islamic State. On Thursday, the House passed a bill containing impossibly onerous yetting procedures for new refugees from Syria.

What does this mean? What process do refugees go through to come to the US?

The American character is being tested. Will we hew to our long tradition of being a beacon of hope for those chased from their homelands?

Why are people being chased from Syria?

I have always believed that the United States is a place of refuge for those escaping persecution, starvation or other horrors that thankfully most in America will never experience.

Is this argument? Does America should be a place/safe haven. I still believe.

First, we need to put the numbers in perspective. In the case of Syrian refugees, the United States has agreed to accept about 5 percent of those fleeing the Islamic State, also known as ISIS. They will be allowed in our country only after the federal government conducts a robust and rigorous screening process. The numbers arriving in any one state are small: From Oct. 1, 2014, to Sept. 30, 2015, 25 Syrian refugees settled in Washington State.

Evidence that the US is careful who is admitted to US.

These numbers are confusing

Nevertheless, many of my fellow governors have been quick and loud in proclaiming their states off limits to Syrian refugees — even though governors lack authority to close state borders to refugees. They spoke before knowing what the review process entailed, and in some cases punctuated their comments with divisive and misguided rhetoric that appeared to saddle all Syrians with the crimes of the Islamic State.

Inslee is critical of other governors who are trying to prevent refugees from entering their state.

The House bill, which President Obama has said he will veto, would essentially halt the resettlement of refugees fleeing Syria. That's a mistake driven by fear, not sound policy making. It doesn't offer meaningful improvement to what is already a rigorous screening process, but would effectively close our borders to the victims of the Islamic State.

Are governors afraid of terror attacks? Do refugees commit many attacks?

Call to action

I have called for a different approach. I told Washingtonians that I wouldn't join those who wanted to demonize people because of the country they flee or the religion they practice. I will uphold our reputation as a place that embraces compassion and equality and eschews fear mongering.

Figure 5.3
Cris's Annotated Press Release

Above is the screen projection of my annotated press release. I don't talk about all my annotations, but I want students to see a variety of questions and connections. I read aloud the first few lines and share what my inner voice says as I read.

"Hmm . . . this is written by the governor of Washington State. I think he is a Democrat. It was written in November of 2015, so President Obama was in office. But the week before this was written there were coordinated terror attacks in Paris that killed a lot of people. If I remember correctly, around this time, there were mass shootings at a café and another at a concert. Hostages were taken, and suicide bombers killed themselves at a soccer match. The Islamic State took credit for the attacks. Is that ISIS? I wonder if this article was written because people are fearful that refugees might be terrorists?"

As I think aloud, I'm trying to not only show different ways to "talk back" to text but also build background knowledge so students have context for the op-ed piece that will follow.

I model my curiosity, share background knowledge so kids have context, identify confusion, and model how I infer meaning as I read the first few paragraphs aloud. I point out that I've circled words I don't know so I can determine if I need to know them to make sense of the piece. I stop to share a little more thinking: "I wonder what 'onerous vetting process' means. Does Congress want to make laws so strict that it is impossible for refugees to come to the US?"

I look up and the class is staring at me. "So, what do we write?" asks Johnny.

"Don't write anything yet. I want you to notice how I wonder about parts I don't get, and that I ask questions about parts that I am curious about. In a minute, you'll get a chance to practice asking questions you care about."

Johnny shrugs his shoulders and I continue to read aloud the second, third, and fourth chunk. I stop and think aloud about the numbers in the fourth chunk: "Let's see, the way this is written is confusing. I think it says that between the years 2014 and 2015, Washington State took in twenty-five refugees. That doesn't sound like a lot to me. What is the big deal about twenty-five people entering the state? I wonder how the US checks out, or 'vets,' refugees so we know they aren't entering the country to do harm?"

Kids wait for me to answer my own questions. But instead of answering them, I label my thinking by telling them that I ask questions that I don't know the answers to, and the questions that I am most curious about help me decide what text I will read to build my background knowledge. "OK," I say. "Now, it's your turn. I want you to read Inslee's op-ed from the *New York Times,* and as you read, jot down anything that you have a question about. If it is a word you don't know, just circle it and I'll know what you mean. If you don't understand why something is happening, see if you can ask a question. While you are reading and annotating questions that you don't know the answers to, I will come around to see what you think about the piece."

After about six minutes of reading and annotating, student voices start bubbling up. It's my signal that it's time for them to discuss. "When you are ready," I say, "turn to your elbow partner and share a piece of thinking that you care about."

The room is oddly quiet. They are testing me. If they don't talk, do they think I will? To avoid the trap of taking over the class, I head to a table at the back of the room and kneel down next to Luis. Once I start to confer with him, I can hear discussions beginning. "So, Luis, what are you wondering?" He shrugs his shoulders. "OK, look at your annotations." Unfortunately, he doesn't have anything written. He looks at me with an embarrassed look. "No problem," I say. "As you read, was there a question that popped into your head?"

"Yeah, this part." He points to the paragraph that talks about tourist visas. "How come it's easier to get to the US on a visa than it is to become a citizen?"

"Great question," I say. "Write that down. Your question might drive your research and even be a way to start your open letter." Luis doesn't know it yet, but more terror attacks are committed by people who overstay their visas than by refugees. Before I leave his table, I ask Luis if he thinks he can jot down one or two more questions he has about the piece. He nods his head, and I walk away knowing that if I can get all the kids to ask questions they care about, it will help them sift and sort the nonfiction offerings they will get tomorrow.

As they read the op-ed, I want students to notice three things:

- The assigned writing type is an example of something that exists in the world, and that all kinds of people use this genre to share their thinking and/or impact others.

- Good writers study what other writers do to inform their own writing.

- Quality work happens when creators know what success looks like. It happens when a writer is a clear communicator, and they can move readers to think in new ways.

Once students have read the op-ed for the gist, they read it for craft. When handing out the learning target rubric, I tell students, "Now we are going to analyze the writing to see what the author did well and see what he could do better." Students give me a blank stare. I continue explaining, "We are going to use the learning target rubric to look for the parts that are done well and notice parts that are boring." Not surprisingly, they are excited to be the ones critiquing the writing.

Using the learning target rubric to study this mentor text will help students have a clearer idea of what they want their own writing to look like. First, though, I want to flip their role from students to evaluators. This shifts the locus of power. Instead of being at the mercy of the evaluation, the shoe is on the other foot. They get to be the ones who evaluate the writing—something that I want them to do regularly when they read and work on their own drafts.

Working Smarter, Not Harder, with Learning Targets

In *So What Do They Really Know?* (2011), I write about how teachers can assess in ways that immediately inform instruction and lead to quality of students' work. Years ago, I learned from students that feedback too late is useless. Before using learning targets, grading was a nightmare. I'd spend weekends trying to write useful comments on horrible writing only to have students throw their work in the trash when I passed it back Monday morning. They had no idea how hard I tried to give them useful feedback. I'd fumble for the words to justify the grade, trying to preserve academic integrity without discouraging students' desire to write. The writing didn't get better and students were angry that they didn't figure out what I wanted. Especially the students who were used to turning in their first drafts as their final drafts.

On the next page is an example of my feedback before I knew about the power of learning targets. Remembering the wise words of Don Graves, I complimented something about the writing and then asked a question. But after that, the feedback I gave was a waste of time. You'll notice I wrote an inane comment about spelling and punctuation to justify the grade and gave no useful feedback on how to improve. Finally, I randomly assigned the student 80 points.

No wonder students' writing didn't improve! I'm embarrassed by my feedback because it was so ineffectual. I didn't want to discourage the student from trying again, but the quality of work was terrible. I wrestled for probably ten minutes trying to figure out what to write for my final comments. Ten minutes doesn't seem like a long time until you multiply it by thirty students. Then it adds up quickly.

Sure, I used rubrics. I even shared them with students before the assignment was due. They had time to read the rubric and ask questions about parts they were unclear about. Rubrics were also a way for me to justify points when students were unhappy about their grades. When students complained, I simply reminded them, and their parents, that we had "discussed" the requirements in class long before the assignment was due.

However, there are unintended consequences with this approach. One, the kids didn't want to read the rubric, let alone ask questions about it. And two, I wasn't even sure what the rubric meant. When I did my own assignment, and strove for success, I couldn't even hit a "four" on the rubric. So, I tried to find examples of what a "four" would look like, but not even Pulitzer Prize-winning columnists achieved the highest score on most rubrics. There were just too many verbs and adjectives for students to hit the criteria of success!

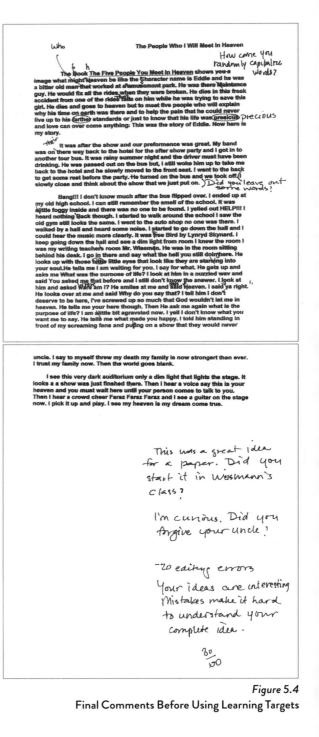

Figure 5.4
Final Comments Before Using Learning Targets

Well-written learning targets guide students toward high-quality work, and they give teachers a way to focus their feedback so they aren't spending hours writing comments to justify the grade. When targets are paired with high-quality models, they give students an idea of what success looks like. To help me decide on the criterion, I find authentic examples of the work, like Jay Inslee's editorial, that I want students to create. I analyze the qualities of the exemplar work, and then I do my own assignment to help me identify the learning targets I want students to focus on. When I follow these steps, I can see where the standards come from; they emerge as important qualities of writing one uses to communicate with a reader instead of a checklist of qualities to "cover." Some genres lend themselves to certain standards. The key is that students have the opportunity to write in a variety of genres to communicate their thinking over the course of a year.

Once I decide on the targets that I want students to meet, I share the models and mentor texts with them so they can see concrete examples of what I want them to do. When students write a first draft, usually responding to one of the provocative questions, I can see what they know and need. This helps me begin designing minilessons that will help students meet the targets.

When I build in a few opportunities on my planning calendar for students to revise, I can give them connected feedback in between drafts. Students also use the targets to tell me what they need. This helps me differentiate my instruction and gently remove the mask of minimal effort from kids who aren't sure how to re-enter their writing. These few steps have virtually eliminated the dreaded weekends of grading horrible writing.

The Open Letter Learning Target Rubric

After students do their initial draft of the open letter, and I have a chance to quickly look through them for patterns of need, it's time to introduce the learning target rubric. Notice that I've focused on a few aspects of quality and not loaded students down with numerous vague tasks that they need to include in their final draft of writing. (See Figure 5.5.)

Like my dad labeling the mechanics of McEnroe's serve, the learning target rubric identifies criteria for high-quality work. Each target gives students a learning goal to shoot for. It also offers them something to refer to as they decide what they will revise for subsequent drafts. Unlike the old days, when I spent precious time trying to justify a grade, the learning target rubric gives students and me something to reference when receiving and giving specific feedback.

To move students beyond the barf draft, I ask them to annotate the learning target rubric with questions and concerns about what I'm asking them to do. I want to make sure they know what each target means.

Vanessa's annotated learning target rubric gives me insight into what see needs. It also helps her tell me where she might get stuck. As an English learner, she finds several of the nouns and verbs confusing. When she circles the words and adds annotations, she helps me see what she needs.

At the end of the day, I quickly look at students' annotated learning target rubrics. With a pencil and paper in hand, I jot down patterns I notice. Most kids don't know what the word *embed* means. No one knows what a *call to action* is. Everyone has limited background knowledge about the Syrian refugee crisis. A few kids don't annotate their learning target rubric at all. It's OK. I feel confident that any minilesson I choose for the next day will meet at least one of their needs.

There are lots of instructional paths that I can take. There isn't one right skill to model, or one right text to choose for the minilesson. Over the course of the unit, students will certainly need to read historical and informational text to give them context. Current events will help them identify issues surrounding the crisis. All of this reading will build

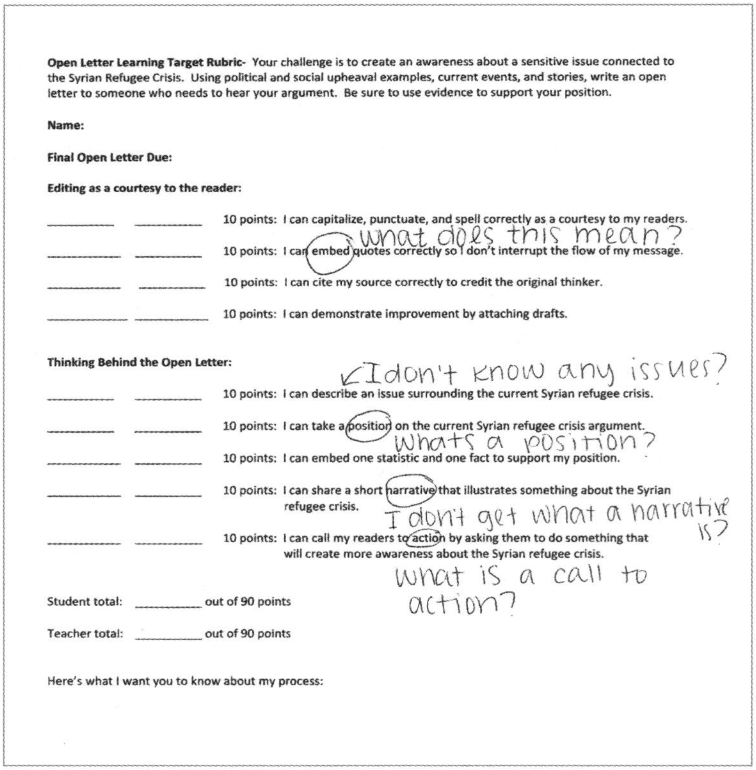

Figure 5.5
Vanessa's Annotated Learning Target Rubric

their background knowledge so they can take a position to argue. While students read, I confer and use small-group instruction to model different ways for students to get unstuck.

Similar to how I modeled reading Inslee's press release and editorial, I also show students how I read the learning target rubric. I want students to begin using the rubric to notice and label the writer's craft moves. I model a difficulty many students in the past have struggled with as I think aloud, "I always wonder how authors support their argument. So, as I read Inslee's op-ed again, I want to notice how he crafted his position and then used evidence to support it."

Karissa jumps in: "Yeah, I want to know how to do that too. My teachers tell me to do that all the time and I'm not really sure what it means."

"Great, Karissa, let me know what you figure out. You and I can compare what we notice." I also suggest that students pay attention to how the author embeds story and historical information. A few students nod their heads. Others are clueless. It's time for me to stop talking about my process so they can start focusing on theirs.

Over the next two weeks, in the spirit of interleaving instruction, I ask students to return to the Inslee editorial as well as others that I have found, so that they can continue to notice writer's craft. One-and-done attempts at reading and writing complex text are rarely enough for students to produce quality work.

The learning target rubric identifies components that students will need to include in their own writing. Comparing the learning target rubric to strong and weak models helps students identify what makes a piece of writing interesting, confusing, or boring to read. It also helps them decide what they want to try. For now, I ask students to focus on the second half of the learning target rubric, "Thinking Behind the Open Letter." I point out that of course in the Inslee piece conventions like spelling, capitalization, punctuation, and grammar are correct because it was published in the local paper, as well as in the *New York Times*.

As students work, I confer and snoop on their thinking. I notice that Vanessa has only annotated the first page of the op-ed. It's clear from her annotations that she is trying to figure out what each of the learning targets looks like in an authentic op-ed. She is able to identify the argument. She starts to notice how the author supports his position with statistics, but detects that he hasn't identified his source for facts. When I confer with her, she tells me that she is trying to figure out how to embed evidence and give credit to the original source.

After analyzing the mentor text using the learning target rubric, it's time for students to work on their next draft. With a specific purpose and audience in mind, students can now decide which target to work on to make their writing better. I pass back their barf drafts with a few initial comments. Devon reads what I wrote and then turns to the student next to him, pointing to my comment: "What's this supposed to mean?"

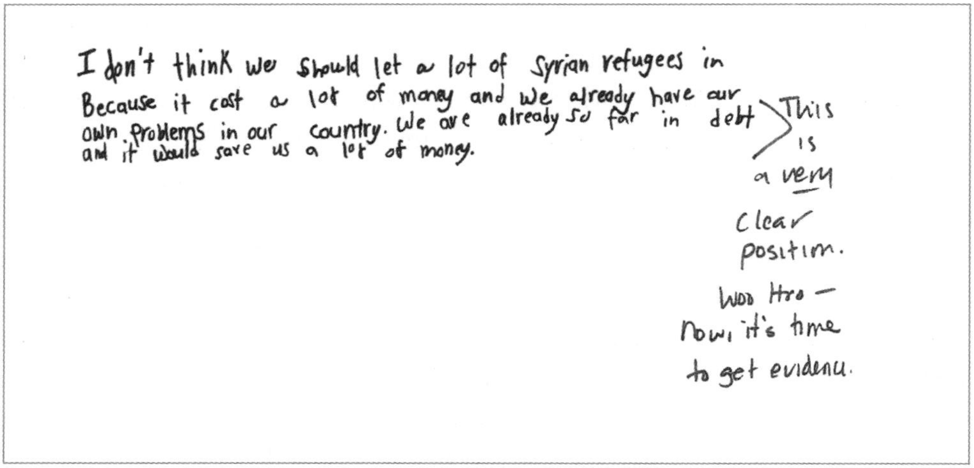
I don't think we should let a lot of Syrian refugees in Because it cost a lot of money and we already have our own problems in our country. We are already so far in debt and it would save us a lot of money.

This is a very clear position. Woo Hoo — Now, it's time to get evidence.

Figure 5.6
Devon's Barf Draft

Devon only took a couple of minutes writing his first draft. As a comfortable wearer of the mask of minimal effort, he thought he was finished. After studying the learning target rubric, he started to realize that he had more writing to crank out. Like everyone else in the class, he needed support for his argument. It's clear that when he wrote his first draft, he wasn't sure what I expected. I want students to be clear early on about the specifications of the assignment. They need to know at the beginning of the unit, before they waste time trying to guess what I want, which aspects of writing I will be assessing. Referring Devon back to the learning target rubric will help him see that he has completed one aspect of the assignment but there are several other additions he needs to make.

I continue to pass back drafts and explain that before the next one is due, students will know a lot more about writing open letters. While reading their first attempts, I limit myself to jotting only one or two pieces of feedback on their writing. It's more important that I notice what they can already do, name it for them, and then identify something that they need next to grow. Once I've identified a few patterns of need, I begin designing minilessons. Here are a few examples of what students needed:

Minilessons Students Need to Keep Going (collected from reading students' barf drafts):

- *How do I take a position?* Many students struggle with this because they need more information on the issue or topic. I can show mentor texts of op-eds and open letters to point out where the position is stated. Bringing in a variety of positions will help students see that I'm not looking for them to agree with me and that any position can be taken as long as it can be supported with evidence.

- *What can I use for evidence?* Mentor texts can also be used to show students different kinds of evidence (statistics, facts, data, expert testimony) and how to find credible sources.

- *How do I cite my sources?* Students won't use footnotes or a works cited page for an open letter, so I will need to model different ways they can quote sources. To ensure they don't plagiarize, students will need to know that it's necessary to cite their sources if they use the thinking of others as evidence.

- *How do I tell if a source is credible?* Certain sources, like self-published materials, should be avoided. Students need to be able to distinguish scholarly versus nonscholarly websites and books, and consider the timeliness of the source. (Students can look at the URL and research organizations that are quoted in their source.)

- *How do I embed evidence?* I first need to define *embed* for students. Using the mentor texts, I will show how other authors embed evidence. I can point out that a writer creates context for the reader before the source is added and then helps the reader make a connection to the point they are trying to make.

Not all students need every one of these minilessons. Taking an entire day of instruction to model each one in isolation so that students can practice all of these skills would be a waste of time. I try to be flexible and fluid about when I offer minilessons and who I "invite" to small-group instruction. These minilessons can happen with individuals, small groups, or the whole class, depending on students' needs. This is another way I get students to take off the mask of minimal effort. When they see that a lesson is designed specifically for them, based on their actual work, they are more willing to revise.

Heading back to the classroom the next day, I have lots of choices on what I can model. For the students who think they are finished after only one draft, I want to be sure I check in with them to see if they know what to do next. Until he got my feedback the following day, Devon was pretty sure his barf draft was good enough. During work time, I notice him on his computer. "What are you working on?" I ask.

"Just finding evidence," he says.

"Evidence for what?"

"Well, I thought that all I had to do was give my opinion, but you wrote back that I needed to find evidence. I found out how much debt the US is in, but I can't seem to find how much it costs to have refugees here."

We brainstorm a few topics he can search, and I share some different ways to tell if a source is credible. Before heading to the next student, I thank him for digging back into his writing. Three days later, students turn in their next draft. I come to Devon's. He's not there yet, but this piece has come a long way from his first draft.

> - The us is $19.19 billion in debt
> - The us pays $1.8 billion annually for refugees
>
> In Syria there is a civil war like crisis and it all started in 2011, when teenagers protested against their leader Bashar al Assad and they spray painted a wall saying it's not fair and they don't want him their leader. Then Bashar put them all in jail and tortured them. The parents and other people didn't like it and were very angry. The protesting and Bashar got scared and started killing his people.
> *bombing*
>
> I don't think we should let a lot of Syrian refugees in the U.S because it cost a lot of money and we already have our own problems in our country. We are already so far in debt and it would save us a lot of money to bring in a lot less refugees.
>
> The U.S is $19.19 trillion in debt and our government pays about $1.8 billion every year. Welfare costs about $867,004,000 a year just on refugees and $71,275,000 a year on education. *(Source)*
> *Is this for all people or refugees.*
>
> Tovani I need help getting all my thoughts down and sounding more humane because I still want to help all the refugees and I feel horrible that this stuff is happening but I have a strong opinion to focus on our own country
> *Ask me about the U.N article. Maybe you can ask the UN to do more.*
>
> *Maybe you could suggest something that refugees could do in addition to paying back their loan.*

Figure 5.7
Devon's Second Draft

From day one, I try to set the expectation that revision will be a big part of the work we do in class. I build time into my lesson planning so that students get feedback in between drafts. In school, we expect kids to take academic chances all day long. Often when they take these chances, there isn't enough time or support built in for revision, which causes students to fail if they can't produce quality work on their first attempt. After failing multiple times, students start to give up, or they resort to cheating, or refuse to revise and redo. Putting on the mask of minimal effort keeps kids safe. When teachers build in opportunities for students to get feedback to the targets before they revise, they experience increments of success, which keeps them going.

It's easy to assume that students who do the bare minimum are lazy. This isn't always the case. To figure out how to remove the mask of "one-and-done," I think about what I would need to write a high-quality paper. First, I'd need an example of what I'm trying to write or create. Next, I'd need a reason to revise. If I'm going to go to all the trouble to redo something, I need an audience to share the work with. I'm really busy, so if there isn't some time built in for revision, I will just slapdash the task to get it over with. Finally, in between my revisions, I'd need some specific feedback so I can improve the work.

Real Work: The Need for Audience and Authenticity

If you really want to ramp up students' urgency to revise and produce quality work, you need an authentic audience. Providing an audience for students to share their thinking requires a little bit of planning, but it's well worth the effort.

When I'm stuck on what I want students to make or do to demonstrate that they've hit the targets connected to standards, I notice what professionals in the world outside of school do to share their thinking. What do they create? How do they share their knowledge? I collect and photograph their products and jot down authentic demonstrations of understanding. I ask myself, *Who are the professionals who engage is this type of work? What do they make and do?* When students who wear the mask of minimal effort have the opportunity to create and engage in the work of professionals, they are more eager to do the work of school.

To get ready for the Awareness, Empathy, and Action Summit I contact churches, nonprofits, government agencies, and universities in the area to invite people to attend. I want the guests to listen to students and share their perspectives on the current refugee crises. I work hard to find a diverse panel of guests so students see themselves reflected in the experts. Once the invitations have been sent, there is no turning back. For students to be prepared for this real-world audience, everything they do in class will be in preparation for that second-to-last day of the quarter, when they will be the masters of their own fates.

A Few Public Forums That Exist in the World

Expert panels
Roundtable discussions
Summits
Soapbox speeches
Blogs
Submissions to local papers

There is important work for teenagers to do. They need to create awareness around issues, engender empathy, and take action. When a topic hits close to home, I want them to see how it will impact their pocketbooks, safety, and well-being. Only then, will they have a purpose for the learning. Kids want to do work that matters, and when we give them the chance to do it, minimal effort turns into maximum impact—for learners and their communities.

What Works? Five CYA Strategies That Remove the Masks of Minimal Effort:

1. Do your own **Tasks.** Doing both summative and formative "makes and do's" will help you:

   - determine whether an assignment is worthy of students' **Time**;

   - judge how much time is required to think, practice, and create; and

   - decide which models and mentor **Texts** are needed to provide examples so students can get unstuck.

2. Use real-world writing to craft product-based learning **Targets** and rubrics. Spend **Time** unpacking the rubrics and using them to assess and critique a variety of strong and weak models so students start to internalize what high-quality work looks, sounds, and feels like.

3. Start with a compelling **Topic** and plan backwards from a combination of authentic products and performance-based assessments (**Tasks**). If you want students to be able to _____, then they must _____. In order to _____, they must _____.

4. Build **Time** into your calendar for students to write and revise in class. From day one, set the expectation that revision will be a big part of the work they will do. Build this time into your lesson planning so that students get feedback in between drafts.

5. **Tend** to students by noticing patterns in their daily work. Design minilessons using what you notice, and find models to show students what the criteria of success look like. Notice what students can already do in their work, and what they need next to grow. Once you've identified a few patterns of confusion, you can decide what minilessons you will do for the entire class, small groups, and/or individuals.

Chapter 6
The Mask of Invisibility

Years ago, sitting in the second row of my high school's theater, I anxiously awaited my professional hero, Don Graves. His new book, *Testing is Not Teaching* (2002), had just come out, and Don had been visiting a local elementary school earlier in the day. After I reassured him that the secondary teachers in my building wanted to fight back against the tyranny of testing, he graciously agreed to squeeze in an afternoon meeting with the English department.

Don opens the conversation with a task. He asks everyone to take out a blank sheet of paper. "When you're ready," he says, "pick a class and see if you can list every student's name. Then, next to each name, jot down one or two things you know about that student."

I decide to use my fourth hour, a reading intervention class.

I look down at my list of names. I'm four short. *Who have I forgotten? Let's see, I've got Connor, can't forget him. I've got Luis and Megan. I've got Oscar and Manny.* It's late September. *By now,* I berate myself, *I should be able to list every kid without looking at a roster.*

In my head, I picture the clusters of desks that make tables in the room. Starting with the ones close to the board, I see Morrissa, Maria, Thalia, but I can't picture the fourth student who sits with this group. I pull up my class roster to see who I'm missing. Of course, Mercy! She's so quiet. My eyes continue down the list, and I realize that I've also left off Ben and Simon. They sit at the back of the room and would probably melt into the bookshelf if they knew how. I'm missing one more. My eyes continue down the roster, and at the bottom I see Alexandra's name. Yes! Alexandra, always deferential and wearing half a smile.

I let out a sigh. Why can't I remember Mercy, Simon, Ben and Alexandra? What is it about them that makes them so easy to forget? They are all quiet in class, but is that because they are introverts or because they are confused or bored? Is it because they lack confidence and don't believe that their thinking matters? Are they afraid of mispronouncing a word and being laughed at? Or . . . is it because I haven't bothered to look beyond their silence?

We all have a few students who wear the mask of invisibility. If that mask is never taken off, of course we can't remember who they are. To be honest, kids like Mercy and Ben weren't on my radar because I figured, if they were quiet and seemingly on task, I could put my efforts elsewhere. It wasn't until teachers started observing my classroom and asking me questions about these quiet students that I started to wonder, too.

"What do I do with the students who don't talk?"

"How do I know what they understand?"

"I have several girls who don't say a word. What do I do with them?"

Yeah, what do we do about the kids who don't give us any verbal indications of their thinking? Unlike our students who wear the masks of anger or class clown, these students rarely give us any trouble with behavioral engagement. But how do we know they are emotionally and cognitively engaged?

Talking Isn't the Only Way to Show Thinking

I've always been attracted to introverts. Maybe it's because I like to make them laugh or prod them into letting me into their bubble. As an extrovert, I respect the power that introverts hold. I love how "stealth" they are—carefully observing what happens around them, holding their cards close to the vest, so others aren't sure of their next move. They don't nag for attention, and I'm often the one who gets to choose if I engage or ignore them. This is all fine and well in adult social circles, but in the classroom, this is a problem. Kids who wear the mask of invisibility can get lost in the shuffle, slip through the cracks, and if the teacher doesn't care or ask to see their thinking, they may not grow as readers and writers. I am not an advocate of "making" kids talk or changing introverts into extroverts. I am interested in giving all learners, even the ones who wear the mask of invisibility, a way to show what they know and need next to grow.

Student talk is a powerful way to see understanding. It's also something that doesn't take hours to grade. Teachers can quickly notice patterns and misconceptions and promptly give feedback when necessary. Unfortunately, if everyone talks at once, it's easy to miss a lot of great thinking. I also have to be aware of students who don't like to talk in class, who would rather put on their mask of invisibility and let others do the conversing. To teach students well, I have to know them well, and I don't mean by testing the heck out of them. I need to provide multiple ways for learners to show me their thinking, and talk is only one way to see it.

So, what do we do with students like Mercy, Ben, Simon, and Alexandra? How do we get students like them to be more visible? It's exhausting trying to make someone talk who doesn't want to. And when I do try to make them talk, I usually lose the power struggle. When students don't talk, I have to find other ways to know what these quiet observers understand. When I can see their thinking, I can adjust instruction and differentiate for their needs. Providing different options for students to show their learning not only gives me a way to adjust instruction, it also helps students hold their thinking as they construct meaning.

Making the Invisible Visible

I pull up a chair next to Alexandra. I can see my proximity makes her cringe a little, so I back up a bit. "Hi Alexandra, how's it going?"

"Fine."

"What are you working on today?"

"This." She slides her free choice novel my way.

"Great, do you like the book? Do you have any thinking you want to share?"

"No."

"No, you don't like the book or no, you don't have any thinking to share?"

"I don't have any thinking to share."

"Is the book too hard?"

"No."

For two weeks, this is how conferences go with Alexandra. Every word out of her mouth is like pulling teeth. One day, out of frustration, I finally say to her, "Look, Alexandra, I know you don't like to talk in front of the class, and you don't have to. But if I'm going to help you get smarter, I have to be able to see what you get and what confuses you. I need a way to see your thinking."

Pausing, I hope that Alexandra's silence is her way of contemplating my dilemma. Naturally, she doesn't say anything, so I continue. "How can you show me what is going on in your head as you read and write? Can you choose a think-sheet that might hold your smartest thinking?"

"Probably," she says.

"Which one do you want to use?"

"I don't know."

"Do you want to go over to the thinksheet files and see if one grabs your attention?" Since she will do anything to get me away from her, she agrees and heads over to the files.

Thinksheets are tools that let students enter into the learning process wherever they are. They are simply designed pages that give students a place to hold thinking as they make sense out of new learning. Since snippets of thinking are held on the thinksheets, it's easy for students to share their thinking with me without having to talk in small groups or in front of the whole class. For the time being, students who are more comfortable wearing the mask of invisibility can be seen by me but not by their peers. Eventually, especially when I give them feedback on the thinksheets, many quiet students start to feel more comfortable sharing thoughts with their peers. With thinksheets, the invisible becomes visible.

I recognize the importance of talk and how it helps learners construct meaning. So I never give up on quiet observers talking in small or whole groups. My goal is to help them appreciate that their thinking matters and that in order to get smarter as a community, we need their brains! Often times, thinksheets give students the rehearsal they need to remove the invisibility mask and share their thoughts in front of and with their peers.

What They Are and What They Aren't

When my second book, *Do I Really Have to Teach Reading* (2004), came out, I admit, I occasionally went on Amazon and read the reviews. Most of them were favorable, but one in particular got into my head. The reviewer liked the book and said that they had found it useful, but the complaint was that many of the worksheets in the back of the book were ones already published in *I Read It But Don't Get It* (Tovani 2000). Three aspects of the review bothered me:

> There were no worksheets in the book. ZERO.

> Worksheets typically have one right answer. Thinksheets hold multiple responses and are designed to help students show thinking so their teacher can see what students need next to grow. They are not intended to be isolated activities to keep students busy.

> The thinksheets that the reviewer referred to as *worksheets* were templates that could be altered to meet the needs of different content-area teachers and their students.

Sure, you might be thinking, tomayto, tomahto, but thinksheets nurture student agency and encourage them to be in charge of their own learning. They give students a way to try out new thinking without the worry of always having to know the "right answer."

Thinksheets provide a place for students to

- share questions they are embarrassed to ask in front of others;

- focus on a few aspects of the text that strikes them;

- monitor their thinking and repair meaning when it breaks down;

- reference parts in the text that they want to use later in their writing or discussion;

- hold facts, evidence, and/or plot points to go beyond the literal retelling level and infer meaning;

- choose what they want to focus on, share, or write about;

- track understanding and notice how it grows over time; and

- take safe learning risks.

When it comes to distinguishing thinksheets from worksheets, one isn't necessarily better than the other. It depends on the purpose of the teacher. When I think of a worksheet, I picture a multiple-choice quiz or a fill-in-the-blank activity. When I picture a thinksheet, I imagine a place that invites divergent thinking. Thinksheets help me see all kinds of thinking from all kinds of learners. They help me gauge what students know and need. On the other hand, when I need a quick grade for the gradebook, or I want to assess low-level knowledge, I use a worksheet. I also keep in mind that worksheet responses may have been copied from another student or a website.

When I've asked teachers from all over the country what they think the biggest differences are between thinksheets and worksheets, here's what they most often say:

Thinksheets	Worksheets
• Show students' thinking processes • Illuminate students' needs and misunderstandings • Serve as a stepping stone to more complex thinking and writing • Invite diversity of thought • Honor the values and the current background knowledge of the learner • Fuel discussion and draft writing • Honor Bloom's higher-order thinking skills: synthesis, analysis, evaluation • Support emotional engagement because the teacher can show interest in individual thoughts when she provides feedback • Show growth in thinking over time • Provide clues to students' cognitive engagement • Encourage students to track what and why they think the way they do • Help students track back to how they came to know by identifying evidence or support • Encourage thinking because of multiple entry points • Allow for differentiation because the same thinksheet can be used for the most striving to the most accomplished learner • Allow misconceptions to come out so the teacher can design instruction around clarification • Help the teacher identify patterns of confusion and understanding • Are subjective to grade and usually take more time • Are more fun to grade because there are a variety of responses • Help the teacher collect enough feedback to know where to go the next day	• Honor the right answer and convergent thinking • Are easy to grade • Are easy to copy • Reflect the values of the questioner • Provide feedback when many in the class answer incorrectly • Provide information about knowledge gaps and can be used for summative knowledge mastery • Serve as a quick check to assess a benchmark • Honor one-and-done learning • Honor repetition and drilling of skills • Focus on a "get it done" attitude • Honor emotional engagement for students who like to "get the right answers" • Make it difficult to trace back how students come to know • Don't provide many reliable clues into cognitive engagement • Can be time-consuming to construct • May shut down some students' thinking because they don't know the right answers • Keep some kids "busy"

*For ideas on how to grade and assess thinksheets, see *So What Do They Really Know* (Tovani 2011).

Some kids just tell us what they need, but for others who are unsure, they definitely don't want to telegraph what they don't know to the whole class. Thinksheets help all students take off their masks, but for students who wear the mask of invisibility, they're a way to safely show thinking.

On the thinksheet example below, Natalie, a quiet eighth grader, shares her thinking on a Learning Target Tracker. She responds to the targets by sharing what she thinks it means to be a scientist and what she knows and wonders about kinetic energy. I am surprised by her feisty responses because whenever I've been in her class, she has dutifully done work without making a peep.

I learn a lot about Natalie as a budding scientist. I see from her initial responses to the targets that Natalie is pretty sure science is all about copying the work of another scientist.

Her honest responses give me a heads up that the teacher and I need to help Natalie redefine her idea of what scientists do. We also need to help her see how science fits into her world.

Notice how honest and short my comments are. I'm trying to build emotional engagement with Natalie by acknowledging her honesty with my own. I push back a little by asking her a question that will hopefully point out that there is no need to ask questions you already know the answers to.

Student thinking matters most, and that's why I love thinksheets. They help me see what learners know

Learning Target Tracker How do you want to get smarter? What can you do and what do you need to learn? What do you wonder about the targets?

Daily/Weekly Learning Targets	Reflections:
I can behave like a scientist to figure out the world around me.	They just experiment and thats not very hard.
I can study what other scientists have done to inform what I will do.	Yes, I just have to copy what they have done?
I can ask questions about phenomena that I don't understand. • When I read, I can ask questions I care about and ask ones that I don't know the answers to.	I don't know what phenomena means or is. And I do ask questions but most of the time it is already answered. Isn't it boring to answer questions you already know the answers to?
I can use scientific laws to describe how objects at the macroscopic and microscopic/nanoscopic scale move.	I don't know most of those words.
I can build my scientific background knowledge to explain how and what I observe works.	Why would that affect anything I do? I love that you are asking this question. How does science affect your life?

Figure 6.1
Natalie's Learning Target Tracker

and need immediately, and this guides my instruction. When I give kids a worksheet, I'm expecting a right answer to a question that I think is most important. With worksheets students believe that they have to guess what's in my head if they don't know the answer. Worksheets are also boring to read and grade! Rarely am I surprised by a student's response. When I read thinksheets, students surprise me, in a good way, all the time!

Design Structures That Make Thinksheets Versatile

Teachers can spend hours creating worksheets, and this time often takes away from the most important job of teaching. While serving for years as an English teacher, secondary reading interventionist, and instructional coach, I realized that if I could come up with some variations of the thinksheets that I used in language arts, students would quickly figure out how to use them in their other content areas. If students understood the basic format of a thinksheet in one class, teachers wouldn't have to use instructional time teaching students how to use it in their content area. For example, the structure of the double-entry diary is that the left-hand side of the page captures textual evidence, and the right-hand side holds students' thinking about the evidence. It doesn't matter what text structure one is reading—the format works. This pattern saves teachers prep time creating ways for students to show thinking and class time explaining how to use them. (See examples in Appendix B).

People like patterns. It helps them know what to expect, and when a structure is familiar they can take calculated risks and have more brain space to process new information. Thinksheets' predictable structures honor multiple ways to construct meaning. Students who are quiet or stuck and even the ones who act defiant or apathetic appreciate the predictability of thinksheets and take comfort that there is more than one right answer.

Knowing what to expect from thinksheets and knowing that student thinking will drive my teaching the very next day, helps learners to feel safe so they are more willing to take learning risks down the road. Predictable structures allow for the unpredictable—like student "ah-ha's"—to happen on a regular basis.

I've synthesized my thinksheets to roughly eight structures. I'm sure you've probably seen and used many of them in your practice. These structures are endlessly malleable because they aren't designed to be activities used in isolation, or ways to capture "right answers." The same thinksheets can be used in different content areas with different topics. This saves teachers' time because they aren't spending hours designing review guides or fancy worksheets that students can easily copy off of another students or fill in with very little critical thought.

Eight Go-To Structures for Thinksheets

1. Learning Target Trackers (See Figure 6.1 on page 137.)

2. Provocative Question Reflections

3. Double-Entry Diaries

4. Inner Voice Sheets

5. Synthesis Thinksheets

6. Exit Tickets

7. Vocabulary Builder Sheets

8. Silent Reading Thinksheets

As you look at the examples in this chapter, check out the different ways you are already asking students to hold and show thinking. Would you classify your tools as worksheets or thinksheets? How might you revise or make tweaks to the ones you already have? I bet you'll notice patterns in my designs and be able to create new ones for your students! Your thinksheets will be even better than the ones I've shared. They will help you figure out what YOU want and need to know about your students so that you can serve them well.

Provocative Question Reflections

On the first day of every unit, I ask students to respond to the unit's provocative questions that are most interesting to them. They don't need to respond to every question. I invite them to write to one or two that strike them. Seeing which ones students write to helps me gauge what they are curious about and it helps me see patterns in what they are thinking. As the unit progresses, students will return to their provocative question reflections to add new thinking and notice how their understanding is growing and changing. On page 141 are examples of different units' provocative questions. Before students respond to the question(s) that strike them, I share my initial thinking as a model. I want students to understand that provocative questions don't have one right answer and, therefore, we'll need to return to these all unit long as our thinking grows and changes. Compelling topics require continued reading, writing, and discussing to get smarter about the key issues and complex ideas.

The provocative questions written on anchor charts are posted in the classroom so they are front and center for students to refer to. These questions help students decide what they want to argue and what they will read to build their background knowledge.

Tovani

Provocative Question Reflections: Roosevelt's New Deal
How Do You Want to Get Smarter Today?

Provocative Questions	Reflections
Should the US government help people who are sick, poor, old, handicapped, in the minority, or in harm's way of environmental hazards? Why?	Who helps people now who have no family or financial means?
Can the federal government really make a difference in our day to day lives? Why?	What does the federal gov't pay for now? Public schools, fire and police? (Is that local gov't?)
In your opinion, did FDR's New Deal work?	What exactly was FDR's New Deal? Did his adminstration start social security?
Do we need another *New Deal* today?	Is this like the "Green Deal" I keep hearing about?

Figure 6.2
Provocative Question Reflections—Tovani Model

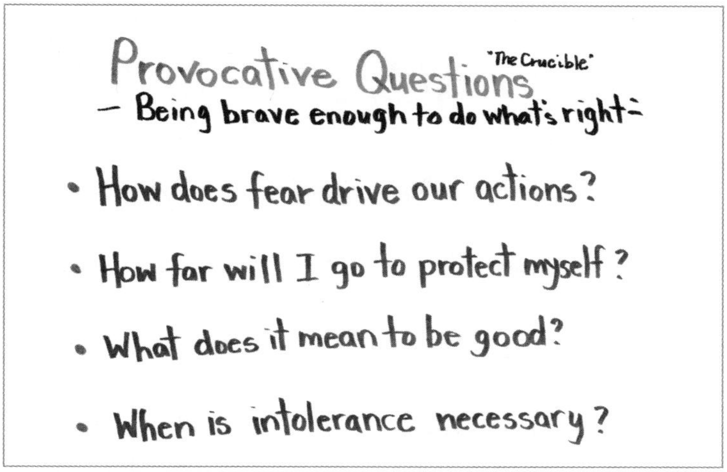

Figure 6.3
Provocative Question Anchor Chart Connected to *The Crucible*

Examples of Provocative Questions

AP Government

- Does the federal government have too much power? Were the anti-federalists right?
- Can they do that? How do the current actions of the president, Congress, and the Supreme Court reflect or conflict with the Founding Fathers' intent for American democracy?
- Is the Constitution still relevant?
- How do I best prepare for the AP test that I'll take at the end of the year?

Eleventh-Grade English *What Are We Fighting For* Unit?

- How does "what I carry" in my heart and head affect how I view the military and the United States involvement in current conflicts?
- Should United States military service be compulsory or voluntary?
- When is killing justified?
- Are the benefits of enlisting in the military worth the risks?
- What "truths" affect a person's decision to enlist?

Eighth- and Tenth-Grade English Social Justice Book Clubs

- How can literature serve as a vehicle for change? Can story move people to take action or think in new ways?

- What is the story I must tell?

- How does where I live, what I look like, and what I believe affect how people treat me?

- How can I be an antiracist?

Eighth-Grade US History

- What forces people to revolt?

- What will people give up to be free?

- What does it mean to be a "good patriot" or citizen?

- What are the effects of colonization on those who are colonized?

- Is America due for a revolution?

Eleventh-Grade Environmental Science

- Will my state be a good place to live thirty years from now?

- Are we doomed if something doesn't change? How might environmental changes affect me?

- How do population pyramids, demographic trends, and recurring patterns help us predict future trends?

- How can a teenager be a citizen scientist?

- Is the data I study plausible, and does it align with what I observe and think to be true?

Ninth-Grade Physical Science

- How can we harness the laws of nature to make us safer, have more fun, and accomplish more work?

- How does understanding Newton's laws inform how we protect athletes, drivers, and passengers from collisions?

- How do I remember what I read? What strategies help me learn vocabulary words?

Seventh-Grade Nonfiction Study Connected to the Environment

- How do people affect the environment?
- What's the big deal about a plant or animal going extinct?
- What can I do to protect the planet—I'm just a kid?

Sixth-Grade Genetics Unit

- What makes me *me*?
- How could a "designer baby" be made? Should a "designer baby" be made?
- How do I know where my traits came from?
- When does human intervention into the basic code of life (DNA) go too far?
- Why do scientists manipulate DNA?

Double-Entry Diaries

Double-entry diaries are another type of thinksheet that I frequently use. As mentioned on page 138, the left-hand side grounds the reader and the teacher in evidence lifted from the text. The right-hand side is a place for learners to react and share their thinking about the textual evidence. Below are four different versions of content-area double-entry diaries. I've added annotations to help you "see" my thinking behind the design of the thinksheet. For **blank versions** of these double-entry diaries, see Appendix B.

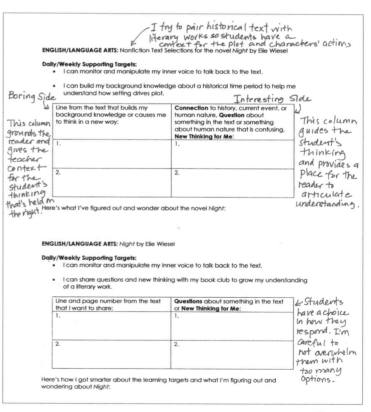

Figure 6.4
English/Language Arts Double-Entry Diaries

I do not create all new learning targets every day. Many are repeated over time and recur with new units of study.

I also post these on the board or make an anchor chart.

SOCIAL STUDIES: World War II European Theater

Daily/Weekly Supporting Targets:
- I can build background knowledge about historical events in order to explain how they impact my understanding of the present.
- I can articulate why the information I am sharing matters.

Some students need a week or more to hit the targets. Others master them in a class period. For this reason, I offer two-four targets a day so students have agency to work on the target they need most.

Record a fact or a piece of information that interests you.	SO WHAT? How does this fact/information help you understand today? Why does this fact/information matter? What questions do you have about this fact/information?
1.	1.
2.	2.

Here's how I got smarter about today's learning targets and WWII:

Environmental SCIENCE: Population Pyramids and Demographic Data

Daily/Weekly Supporting Targets:
- I can predict future trends by analyzing historical data.
- I can ask questions to isolate my confusion.

For more examples of learning targets, see the appendix.

Typically there are five to six rows for students to show their thinking (see the template)

What Do I Observe? Describe what you observe in the data, graph, or table.	What Does it Mean? Record any questions, predictions, or hypotheses you have connected to your observation.
1.	1.
2.	2.

This side is a matched assessment. It pairs with the learning targets and gives students a way to show they've hit the target.

What future population trends can you infer based on the historical data? Reflect on the learning targets. What do you need next?

Figure 6.5
Social Studies and Science Double-Entry Diaries

In the above examples of double-entry diaries, I identify the daily/weekly supporting targets at the top. I want students to keep these in mind as they work so they can reflect on their progress. Double-entry diaries serve as little makes or formative assessments that students use to hold their thinking and demonstrate where they are relative to hitting the targets. They also serve as a place for learners to hold their thinking so they can return to it later to discuss or write about new learning. At the end of each double-entry diary, there is space for students to synthesize their thinking for the day or week. This is another way for me to see if they can articulate new understanding.

When using the environmental science double-entry diary described on page 144, students successfully recorded their observations in the left-hand column but struggled to provide their interpretations in the right-hand column. They weren't asking any questions or making predictions. They weren't connecting what they observed to infer or hypothesize. So, the following day, I gave students a new piece of text to read (Washington State Population Pyramid) and provided another way for them to show their thinking. By specifically labeling ways to interpret the data and listing them below the graphic, I made it easier for students to articulate their depth of knowledge.

Below is a template of typical student response options that are used in language arts. Consider what you want students to pay attention to when they read your content. Then match that thinking with prompts on the right-hand side. The prompts that you suggest should align with how you think as an expert reader of your discipline.

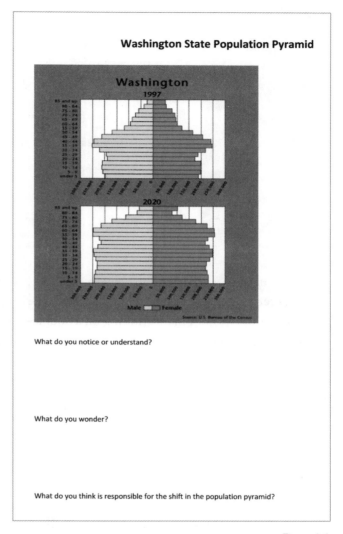

Figure 6.6
Washington State Population Pyramid

Text/page #	Why this text struck me (possible options):
	I made this connection . . . It helped me understand . . .
	I'm wondering about . . .
	This line prompted this sensory image . . . that helped me understand . . .
	This is important because . . .
	This confuses me because . . .
	My inner voice is saying . . .
	Now I'm thinking . . .

Double-entry diaries don't have to be fancy. A simple one can scaffold students who aren't sure how to start a longer piece of writing or participate in a discussion. When students hold their thinking on a double-entry diary like the one below, they can transfer their ideas to more complex writing, like a comparison-contrast essay.

Social justice is...	Social justice is not...

On the next page is an example of another way to use double entries. In black ink is an excerpt from the essay "Self-Reliance" (1841, 133). In blue ink is an example of how I metaphorically unzipped my head to show students different ways to think when reading complex text.

I begin by saying, "I'm going to show you how I get myself ready to read. I can tell this is an excerpt, which is a section of a longer piece. I can also tell the piece was written a long time ago so the language might be old-fashioned. I know from reading other works from Emerson that this will be complex, so I might have to reread parts and ask questions. When I ask myself questions, my brain gets ready to find answers. Spy on my thinking and see what you notice about how I make sense of this piece."

"Self-Reliance" by Ralph Waldo Emerson (1841, 133)

What does the title mean? Self-reliance means being independent. Emerson sometimes writes about nature. So, how does being self-reliant fit with that? I guess in nature you have to be self-reliant or you could die. Hmmm… nature has a lot of different meanings. I wonder if this is about nature like being outdoors or like human nature?

I can't blast through these words without stopping every once in a while. If I do, my "waste of time voice" will turn on and I won't remember what I've read.

Watch how I read this. (I read a section of text and then pause.) I need to reread that line again. Here's what I think it means…Here's what I wonder. I will circle words that I don't know. Maybe someone in my group can help me figure out how they fit.

There is a time in every man's education when he arrives at the conviction that envy is ignorance; that imitation is suicide; that he must take himself for better, for worse, as his portion; that though the wide universe is full of good, no kernel of nourishing corn can come to him but through his toil bestowed on that plot of ground which is given to him to till.

I think the part that I just read says that man is rewarded for his hard work by doing his best. Does he only mean men? Probably not, but because this was written "back in the day," women weren't seen as equals. Does that make sense? I think today we can extrapolate that Emerson is writing about the nature of men and women. I wonder if he thinks all people and socioeconomic classes can understand this. Emerson's audience is probably educated, landowning men. But just to be sure, I'm going to mark this place so I can ask my group members.

Student Annotations

The power which resides in him is new in nature, and none but he knows what that is which he can do, nor does he know until he has tried. Not for nothing one face, one character, one fact makes much impression on him, and another none. It is not without pre-established harmony, this sculpture in the memory. The eye was placed where one ray should fall, that it might testify of that particular ray. Bravely let him speak the utmost syllable of his confession. We but half express ourselves, and are ashamed of that divine idea which each of us represents. It may be safely trusted as proportionate and of good issues, so it be faithfully imparted, but God will not have his work made manifest by cowards. It needs a divine man to exhibit anything divine. A man is relieved and gay when he has put his heart into his work and done his best; but what he has said or done otherwise, shall give him no peace. It is a deliverance which does not deliver. In the attempt his genius deserts him; no muse befriends; no invention, no hope.

Trust thyself: every heart vibrates to that iron string. Accept the place the divine Providence has found for you; the society of your contemporaries, the connection of events. Great men have always done so and confided themselves childlike to the genius of their age, betraying their perception that the Eternal was stirring at their heart, working through their hands, predominating in all their being. And we are now men, and must accept in the highest mind the same transcendent destiny; and not pinched in a corner, not cowards fleeing before a revolution, but redeemers and benefactors, pious aspirants to be noble clay plastic under the Almighty effort, let us advance and advance on Chaos and the Dark....

> *What did you notice? What might you try as you continue reading?*

Patterns Learners Can Count on When Using a Double-Entry Diary

- There will be a place on the left-hand side or below the text for students to copy textual evidence and to identify the words that triggered their thinking. The textual evidence gives others context when they share thinking.

- There will be a place on the right-hand side or below the text for students to show their thinking. This area welcomes open-ended responses. The teacher will provide some options to guide thinking but not restrict it. Students know that any thinking is better than no thinking.

- At the end of every double-entry diary there will be a place for students to reflect and synthesize new learning so the teacher can see what each student knows and needs next.

Inner Voice Sheets

In most cases, it doesn't matter to me which thinksheet or little make students create to demonstrate thinking. What matters is that they have a place to hold thoughts so I can see what they know and need next to grow. If you don't always want to use a double-entry diary, inner voice sheets are another option.

Inner voice sheets are my favorite type of thinksheet because they help dissolve the misconception that meaning is supposed to "arrive" by just pronouncing the words. This style of thinksheet is related to the double-entry diary, but it focuses specifically on students' "inner conversations" as they read. Students record how they are talking back to text. This helps them recognize when they are having a conversation with the text and when their mind is wandering as they think about something unrelated. Inner voice sheets help teachers see how students are accessing the material. When students recognize they are off track, the teacher can model different ways to help them re-engage their meaning-making voice.

Below is an example of Vanessa's thinking as she reads the novel *Refugee* (Gratz 2017). Notice that she has chosen to show me her thinking by chapter.

This style of thinksheet can be used with any grade or reading level. It works with any content area and text structure. It can be used with assigned text or free reading options. Math teachers as well as social studies teachers can use this tool to see student thinking, which will help them clear up misconceptions, repair meaning, and scaffold students to the next level.

I originally designed the inner voice sheet to use with first graders to help them monitor their thinking as they read. When I started teaching high school, I realized it was a tool kids could use instead of annotating directly on the text. Readers identify the chunks of text where they are reading and thinking by filling in the page number(s) on the line at the top of each box. The boxes help readers pay attention to the voice in their head as they read. If students find themselves reading a couple of pages about Syria but are thinking about what they're having for lunch, they can catch themselves before reading too far in the text with their "waste of time voice" on. (For more information on inner voice, see *I Read It, but I Don't Get It* and *Do I Really Have to Teach Reading?* (Tovani 2000, 2004.)

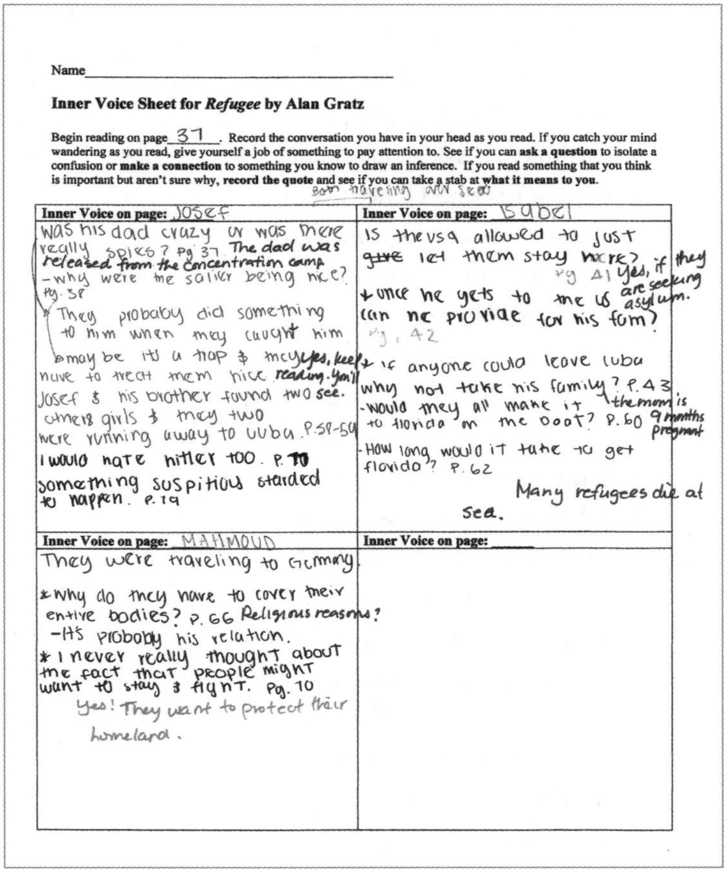

Name______________________________________

Inner Voice Sheet for *Refugee* by Alan Gratz

Begin reading on page 37. Record the conversation you have in your head as you read. If you catch your mind wandering as you read, give yourself a job of something to pay attention to. See if you can **ask a question** to isolate a confusion or **make a connection** to something you know to draw an inference. If you read something that you think is important but aren't sure why, **record the quote** and see if you can take a stab at **what it means to you.**

Both traveling over seas

Inner Voice on page: Josef	**Inner Voice on page:** Isabel
Was his dad crazy or was there really spies? Pg 37 The dad was released from the concentration camp -why were the salier being nice? Pg. 38 They probaby did something to him when they caught him may be it's a trap & they have to treat them nice yes, keep reading. You'll see. Josef & his brother found two others girls & they two were running away to Cuba P.58-59 I would hate hitler too. P. 70 something suspitious starded to happen. P. 19	Is the usa allowed to just ~~give~~ let them stay here? Pg 41 Yes, if they are seeking asylum. * once he gets to the US can he provide for his fam? Pg. 42 * if anyone could leave Cuba why not take his family? P. 43 -would they all make it to florida on the boat? P. 60 the mom is 9 months pregnant -How long would it take to get florida? P. 62 Many refugees die at sea.
Inner Voice on page: MAHMOUD	**Inner Voice on page:** ______
They were traveling to Germany. * why do they have to cover their entire bodies? P. 66 Religious reasons? -It's probably his relation. * I never really thought about the fact that people might want to stay & fight. Pg. 70 Yes! They want to protect their homeland.	

Figure 6.7
Vanessa's Inner Voice Sheet

Inner voice sheets help me collaborate with students in their quest to build understanding. When students share their inner voice, I can answer a question or pose one back. I can clear up a misunderstanding or honor an original thought. By reading students' thinking I can assess, advise, connect, and communicate with students based on what they write. I don't have to respond to every thought. I can pick the ones to respond to that I think will give kids the biggest bang for their comprehension buck.

The big idea behind the inner voice sheet is that students are monitoring their thinking so they don't read with their "waste of time voices" on. When they catch their minds wandering, they go back to the chunk they just read and give themselves a way to talk back to text. Sometimes readers say, "I'm going to reread this chunk and ask a question to clarify confusion." Other times, they may reread to paraphrase or make a connection to something they've learned in class.

The social studies example on page 151 gives students a place to build their background knowledge about the American Revolution. The teacher has organized the boxes around topics that they want students to get smarter about. As students read about these different topics, they have a place to put their questions, their interesting facts, and their new thinking about each box. (See full-sized version in Appendix C.)

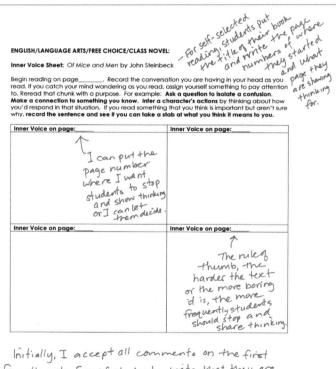

Figure 6.8
Cris's Annotated Steinbeck Inner Voice Sheet
(See a blank full-sized version of this sheet in Appendix C.)

In the math example below (see full-sized version in Appendix C), the teacher has given students different ways to think about how they read and solve math problems. Each box provides a way for students to re-enter the problem and show thinking. Notice the bulleted list of possible ways that students could respond. This is a list of options that teachers might use to guide students' thinking in each of the four boxes.

SOCIAL STUDIES/SCIENCE:

Inner Voice Sheet: Recipe for Revolution

Record the conversation you have in your head as you read the informational text you've selected. If you catch your mind wandering as you read, assign yourself something to pay attention to. See if you can ask a question to isolate a confusion or paraphrase something that you've read. If you read something that you think is important but aren't sure why, record the words and see if you can take a stab at what it means to you.

King George, Lobsterbacks, and Loyalists	Founding Fathers, Firebrands, and Patriots
Taxes, Trouble, and the Tea Party	Ideals, Declarations, and Propaganda

---

MATHEMATICAL INNER VOICE SHEET

Possible ways to record mathematical thinking using pictures, numbers, and/or words:

- Identify skills or processes needed to solve the problem.
- Record what is known about solving the problem.
- Show calculations.
- List questions to isolate confusion.
- Explain why the solution is reasonable and valid.
- Draw a picture or diagram.

As you read the problem, where do you start? What do you know that might help you with this problem?	What questions emerge as you work the problem? Isolate any confusion by asking a question.
Show your steps as you work the problem. Pay attention to your "inner voice" that is saying, "First I should... then I should..."	Based on the steps you took, explain why your answer is reasonable and valid.

When students first use thinksheets, especially the inner voice sheet, they need a model. For some, sharing their first-draft thinking is a new idea. Modeling your thinking helps students to see what to do when their minds wander. Showing different ways you think about text when you read helps them have more ways to talk back to their reading. It's OK to show them your mind wanders. It's great to push back on ideas that you read. Kids love seeing that we have questions and connections about things they might have never thought about.

Below is an example of my thinking on an inner voice sheet that I shared with students in a US history class. As I did on the American Revolution and mathematical inner voice sheets, I gave students four categories to help them determine importance. Students could choose from multiple texts on the topic to build their background knowledge. For this particular unit, the classroom teacher and I wanted students to compare and contrast the New Deal of Franklin D. Roosevelt's time to current policy discussions about the environment.

I shared my thinking on the inner voice sheet during the minilesson so students could see how the thinksheet would help them organize their reading and show the teacher what knowledge gaps needed to be filled.

The goal of inner voice sheets is not to fill out the boxes as fast as possible. Thinksheets are tools to help students hit the learning targets. Sometimes, I will staple

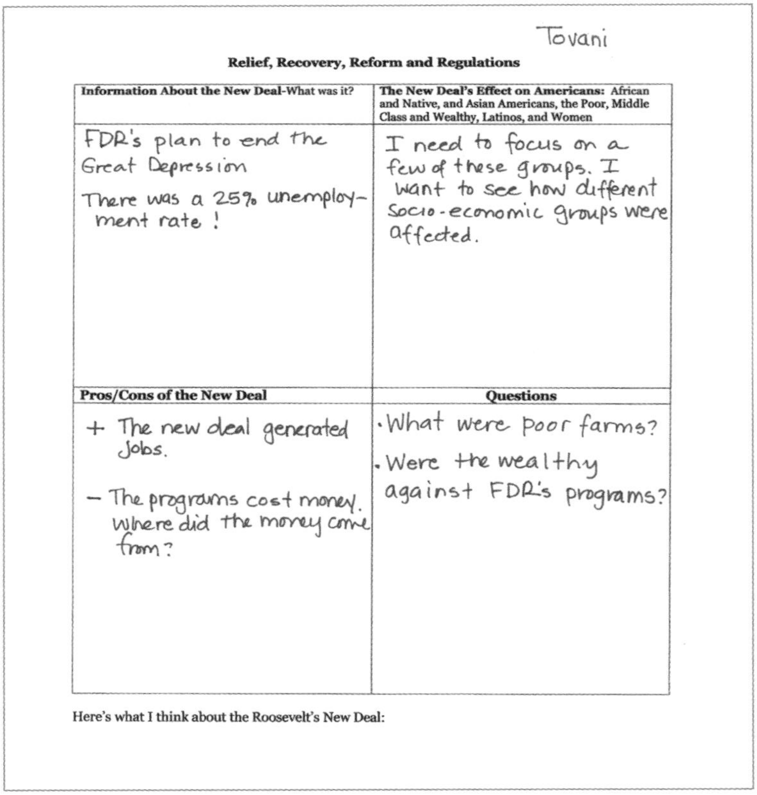
Tovani

Relief, Recovery, Reform and Regulations

Information About the New Deal-What was it?	**The New Deal's Effect on Americans:** African and Native, and Asian Americans, the Poor, Middle Class and Wealthy, Latinos, and Women
FDR's plan to end the Great Depression There was a 25% unemployment rate !	I need to focus on a few of these groups. I want to see how different socio-economic groups were affected.
Pros/Cons of the New Deal	**Questions**
+ The new deal generated jobs. – The programs cost money. Where did the money come from?	• What were poor farms? • Were the wealthy against FDR's programs?

Here's what I think about the Roosevelt's New Deal:

Figure 6.9
Cris's FDR Inner Voice Model

additional sheets so that students can continue adding to their thinking. When students have thinking held on their inner voice sheets, their small-discussion groups thrive, as each student shares what they are wondering and what they have learned.

Patterns Learners Can Count on When Using an Inner Voice Sheet

- Opportunities to pause and record thinking. Students don't need a right answer, but they need to read a little, monitor their thinking, and then jot down what they want to remember. This process helps them monitor when their mind starts to wander.

- If it's students' thinking and voice, it can't be wrong. Students can count on it being okay to write what they think, even if the thinking is off topic.

- The inner voice sheets will be used to improve discussions or bigger pieces of writing.

Synthesis Thinksheets

Synthesis thinksheets are designed to pull students through a process. They help teachers and students notice how thinking grows over time. As students work on their learning, this type of thinksheet serves as a place for them to collect, construct, and revise thinking over the course of a couple of days. Students and the teacher can then track changes in understanding.

Using the model below, students are tasked to read a graph and explain the model using scientific language. Scientists use models to make claims about and

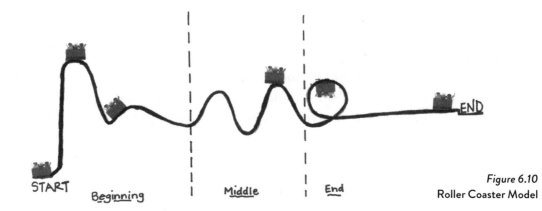

START   Beginning   Middle   End

Figure 6.10
Roller Coaster Model

explain phenomena. The roller coaster model was adapted from the JASON Project to give students a chance to illustrate a roller coaster and then tell the story of the data by looking at it from the beginning, middle, and end of the cycle.

Synthesis thinksheets help students hold and try out their thinking as they gain more information. In the roller coaster example, students move back and forth between the paper model and a computer simulation. Students hypothesize, read, experiment, and then return to their synthesis sheet to revise their claims.

In the example below, eighth graders are learning how to read graphs. The case study is roller coasters and how they move. One of the classroom teacher's yearlong learning targets is that students can use science to explain phenomena. In order for students to engage in the behaviors of scientists versus people who "copy what other people have done," like Natalie thought, I model my thinking about kinetic energy on the same thinksheet that students will soon use.

Figure 6.11
Model of Cris's Kinetic Energy Synthesis Sheet

As you can see, my thinking about roller coasters and kinetic energy is not very sophisticated. But that's okay, because the goal is to model for students, whose thinking in this area is also not very sophisticated, how to make claims, use science vocabulary to explain what they see, and write with sentence stems to explain the phenomena. You will notice in the Beginning box that I wrote and then crossed out words (*higher the hill*), and replaced them with scientific language (*greater the incline*). The science teacher in the room guides students' experimentation and clears confusion, but is careful not to "tell" students the answer. They want students to practice the behaviors of scientists, which means they have to hypothesize, experiment, read, revise, and repeat the cycle.

Once students have a chance to see the model and jot down some initial thinking about kinetic energy and roller coasters, they can build their own coasters using a computer simulation. Students will have several trials to design a roller coaster that doesn't crash through the crowd at the end of the track or get stuck at the bottom of the hill. Notice Olivia and Natalie's thinking as they work to figure out how potential and kinetic energy affect the movement of a roller coaster.

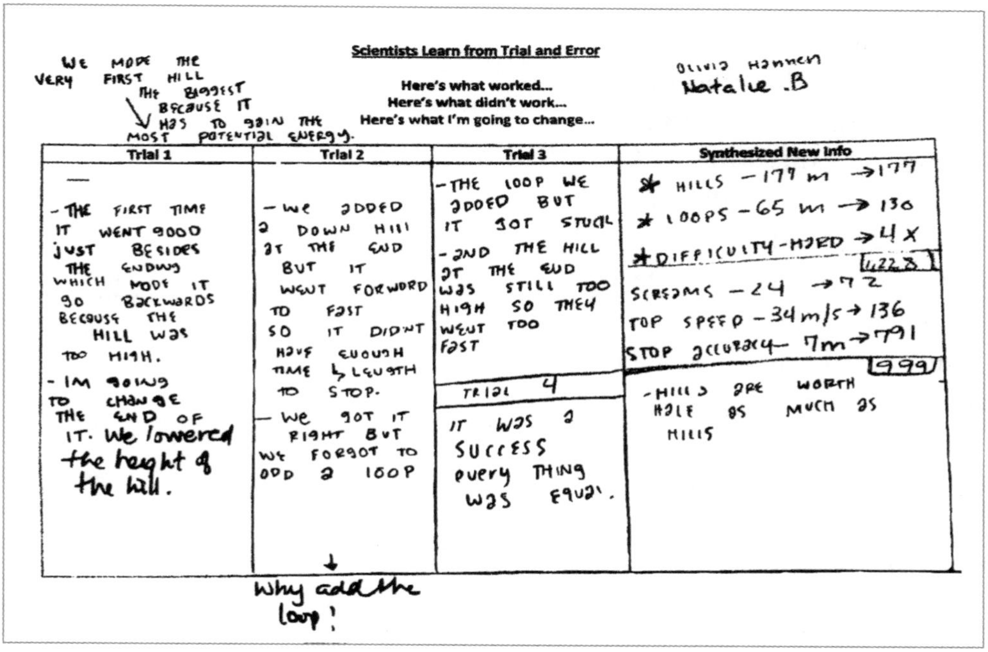

Scientists Learn from Trial and Error

Here's what worked...
Here's what didn't work...
Here's what I'm going to change...

Olivia Hannen
Natalie .B

WE MADE THE VERY FIRST HILL THE BIGGEST BECAUSE IT HAS TO GAIN THE MOST POTENTIAL ENERGY.

Trial 1	Trial 2	Trial 3	Synthesized New Info
— THE FIRST TIME IT WENT GOOD JUST BESIDES THE ENDING WHICH MADE IT GO BACKWARDS BECAUSE THE HILL WAS TOO HIGH. - IM GOING TO CHANGE THE END OF IT. We lowered the height of the hill.	— WE ADDED A DOWN HILL AT THE END BUT IT WENT FORWORD TO FAST SO IT DIDNT HAVE ENOUGH TIME & LENGTH TO STOP. — WE GOT IT RIGHT BUT WE FORGOT TO ADD A LOOP	— THE LOOP WE ADDED BUT IT GOT STUCK - AND THE HILL AT THE END WAS STILL TOO HIGH SO THEY WENT TOO FAST. TRIAL 4: IT WAS A SUCCESS EVERY THING WAS EQUAL.	* HILLS – 177 m → 177; * LOOPS – 65 m → 130; * DIFFICULTY - HARD → 4 X [422.8]; SCREAMS – 24 → 72; TOP SPEED – 34 m/s → 136; STOP ACCURACY – 7m → 791 [999]; - HILLS ARE WORTH HALF AS MUCH AS HILLS

Why add the loop?

Figure 6.12
Natalie and Olivia's Roller Coaster Trial Sheet

Once again, the goal isn't to fill in the columns. The goal is to have a place to hold thinking as it grows over time.

Synthesis sheets help students recognize that complex thinking often doesn't arrive but is constructed over time with multiple opportunities to re-enter the text and task. These thinksheets help students remember what they last thought so that they can continue to develop deeper understanding. In the example below, students are working on a standard connected to theme. On the first day of the study, I model for them using the picture book *Baseball Saved Us* by Ken Mochizuki (1993). I demonstrate how I look for recurring patterns, objects, ideas, and words to discover motifs which help readers develop theme statements.

I read a little and then think out loud for students. Next, they practice what they see me do with a partner using the picture book *Rose Blanche* by Roberto Innocenti and Christophe Gallaz (1985). The synthesis thinksheet in Figure 6.13 guides students to follow the same process I used. This process will work for all literary texts and grade levels that teachers choose to model thinking with. The ultimate goal is to transition students to reading their self-selected novels so that they can practice identifying different literary elements' effects on a reader.

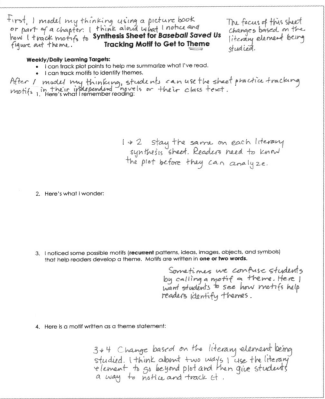

Figure 6.13
Synthesis Sheet for *Baseball Saved Us* by Ken Mochizuki

Patterns Learners Can Count on When Using Synthesis Thinksheets

- There will be a structure to "pull" students through a thinking process.

- Students will have multiple opportunities to go back and retry.

- There will be a place for students to reflect and synthesize thinking over time.

- Questions are honored, as is the identification of confusion.

- Students can use this thinksheet to compare and contrast thinking with peers.

Exit Tickets

Exit tickets are mini-thinksheets that give students an easy way to tell me what they still need at the end of a lesson. Natalie shares how she thinks she got smarter in the exit ticket below:

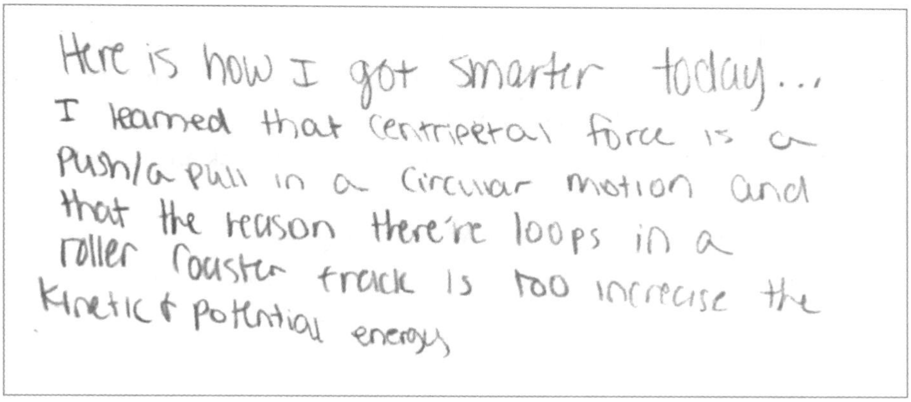

Here is how I got smarter today...
I learned that centripetal force is a push/a pull in a circular motion and that the reason there're loops in a roller coaster track is too increase the kinetic & potential energy

Figure 6.14
Natalie's Exit Ticket Explaining How She Got Smarter

Usually students respond on a sticky note, a half-piece of paper, or a notecard. Exit tickets can show me who is hitting the targets and who isn't. Sometimes I'm not as clear in my instruction as I think I am. Exit tickets help me know when I have to go back and reteach something. They tell me who needs more help and often guide how I design small-group instruction.

Sometimes the reteaching is with the whole class. Other times I can do it with a small group or in a conference.

Students usually complete exit tickets at the end of class. They respond to the learning target, the provocative question(s), or one of the general prompts listed below:

How did you get smarter today?

What do you need next to get even smarter?

What are you still wondering about?

What surprised you today?

What frustrated you today?

What worked for you today?

What are you curious about?

What confused you?

I don't grade exit tickets. I use them to look for growth, new thinking, and patterns of confusion. The exit tickets can quickly tell me something that needs to be cleared up right away. When several students ask the same question, or have the same difficulty or misconception, I know it's time to go back and reteach.

Patterns Learners Can Count on When Using Exit Tickets
- Exit tickets are short and are not graded or personally responded to.

- The teacher will read everyone's exit ticket and use what students write to adjust instruction.

Vocabulary Builders

As an English teacher, I know that having a well-rounded vocabulary matters, but I didn't know how much it mattered until I worked in a high school with predominantly native Spanish speakers. I worked hard to communicate my instruction in both Spanish and English. When a student didn't understand something that I had taught in a minilesson or conference, it wasn't because I didn't know what I was trying to teach. It was because I didn't have the vocabulary to explain my thinking. The more words we know, the more complex thinking we can express.

Below are several examples of vocabulary builders that I use to help students develop their academic and every-day vocabulary. I want learners to go beyond memorizing dictionary definitions so they can use the content-specific terms to describe, explain, and defend their thinking. You will notice three different think-sheet patterns in the samples below that I use to help students construct meaning around new terms, words, and concepts.

In the force and motion example below, I've modeled how I want students to begin showing their thinking. When I constructed the sheet, I identified specific disciplinary vocabulary for students to explore. I don't ask for the definitions. Instead, I want students to activate their background knowledge and tell me what they know about the concept. I also provide a place for them to draw a diagram or give an example of what they know. The last column provides a place for students to ask questions. This gives them an opportunity to isolate confusion and share what they are curious about.

Students can refer to this thinksheet as they add new thinking. The goal isn't for students to rush through and fill out the boxes. This is a tool to hold thinking so that students know where their background knowledge and vocabulary gaps are. It also helps the teacher to see students' misconceptions and where a minilesson or small group might be needed. Students start where they can and then work to build background knowledge in the areas where they need it.

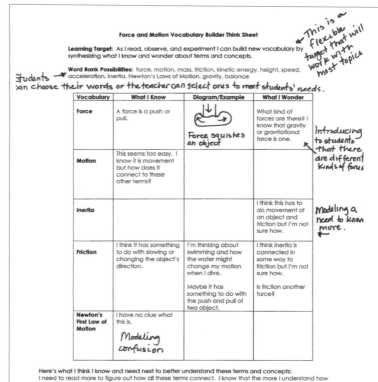

Figure 6.15
Force and Motion Vocabulary Builder Teacher Example

The example below was first developed by social studies teacher Colleen O'Brien. I took her original sheet and made some adaptations. Students are asked to articulate the definition of the terms based on AP US Government's spring test. The concepts are complex, so students also need a place to ask questions and share sketches, examples, and details that will be useful evidence when it comes time to support their written arguments.

Big Ideas in the Constitution	Definition	Questions	Sketches, Examples, Details
Popular Sovereignty	People have power. They use their power to vote for leaders who make decisions for them. If people have this power they believe the government is legitimate. The people are the 'bosses' of the leaders. *(Hobbs and Rousseau)*		
Separation of Powers			
Checks and Balances			
Civilian Control of Military			
Inalienable Rights	The idea that all humans have rights that cannot be taken from them: life, liberty, property, fair trials, free speech, etc... This idea is in the Declaration of Independence, the Preamble to the Constitution, and the Bill of Rights (*John Locke*)		

Figure 6.16
AP US Government Vocabulary Builder

Vocabulary Builder: Connect Two

"Connect Two" thinksheets give students a chance to think about the interconnectedness of content-specific vocabulary. Teachers list words they want students to know in two columns. Students connect any two words they want. The words can be in the same column, different columns, or already connected to another term. This thinksheet's impact is most powerful when students explain *how* the words are connected. The way in which students connect terms helps the teacher flesh out misconceptions and understandings. It also forces students to go beyond dictionary definitions.

Patterns Learners Can Count on When Using Vocabulary Builders

- Students will do more than copy definitions. They will connect new words to existing information.

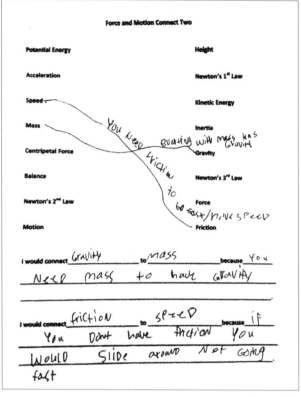

Figure 6.17
Luis's "Connect Two" Thinksheet

- Terms, concepts, and words chosen are ones that matter to the study. Knowing more than the dictionary definition will help students talk about complex ideas in the unit and discipline.

Silent Reading Thinksheets

Silent reading thinksheets are simple ways for students to show and hold their thinking during work time. The purpose of this sheet is to help students remember and reflect on their reading. Often, I show my thinking from a book that I want to feature in a book talk by completing my own silent reading thinksheet. During the minilesson, I share the title, a bit about the plot, and then my thinking about what

I read. When students hold their thinking on this sheet, they can use it to talk in a group or to be held accountable for reading they did at home.

Silent Reading Response Sheet: 67 minutes a day grows good readers!
Date:
Learning Targets:
1. I can increase my reading endurance to finish a book(s).
2. I can monitor my inner voice to share what I remember reading.
3. I can share what I've read to reflect new thinking.

Name: Tovani — Cris

Title of Book Words We Don't Say

Page on which I Started   1   page on which Landed   41   Total pages read   41
                                      9:38   9:50 · 12min
The time I started 11 ℔   The time I stopped 1145   Total minutes read 45 min

How well did you meet the 2nd learning target? What made you stop reading? What do you remember reading? I remember reading about an 11th grader named Joel. He volunteers in a soup kitchen with a girl named Eli, that he has a crush on. Something happened to Joel's best friend, Andy. On page 40, Joel follows a guy from the soup kitchen to his "house." It's a rundown shed on an abandoned farm.

My inner voice got distracted by all the characters. I was having trouble keeping them all straight. I also found myself getting confused on some pages where Joel talks to the reader about his life. I think his diction throws me off. This is something I should mark with a sticky to share with my group.

How well did you meet the 3rd learning target? What were you thinking as you read? Try to write **FOUR** sentences. You might try to: ask questions, make connections, give opinions, share new thoughts, and/or ideas that you think are important.

What happened to Andy? Did he die? If so, how? What's going to happen to Rooster, the homeless guy? I'm trying to keep my eyes out for the social justice issue in this book. Joel seems like a pretty cool kid but I think he has some grief issues he's not dealing with.

Figure 6.18
Silent Reading Thinksheet Model

Patterns Learners Can Count on When Using the Silent Reading Thinksheet

- Students will have a place to track plot in fiction or identify big ideas in nonfiction.

- Students will have a place to share their take on what the reading means to them.

- Students will be expected to read longer over time to demonstrate that their reading endurance is improving. Minutes spent reading is more important than pages read.

Thinksheets provide a gold mine of formative assessment data to help teachers see what learners know and need next. To design them, I think about the feedback I want to get from students to help them grow. I consider how students will hold and show their thinking. I want there to be a place where students can share what they know. If they don't know a lot, I want them to have a place to identify their confusion or ask questions. With thinksheets, the emphasis is on constructing meaning. The goal isn't to complete a thinksheet but to use it to develop understanding. When students have multiple low-stakes ways to show their thinking, they are able to take off any mask they are wearing.

Back to the Big Questions

Let's examine our big questions through the lens of thinksheets. How do they help students who wear the mask of invisibility be known? Don't forget the students who act out, fool around, and avoid work when it's time to get down to business. Thinksheets help them take their masks of disengagement off too.

1. **How do I get students to think for themselves?** Don't teach skills and strategies in isolation. Remember the drunken bears and wedgie story in Chapter 2? Cradle the facts, vocabulary, and skills in a worthy topic. Help students see how their snippets of thinking connect to a bigger idea and the world outside of school. Give students multiple ways to respond. Then respond to back to them. You don't have to write a lot. Sometimes a question or a comment like "Wow, I hadn't thought of that" reassures students they are on the right track.

2. **How do I get kids to care about their learning?** Students care about their learning when they see a purpose for it and have some agency in how to respond. When students see that

their learning connects to something that is valued outside of the classroom, like being able to argue and help others get smarter, they are more motivated to care about the work they are asked to do in school.

3. **What do I do with kids who won't read and write?** Guide students to choose a text that looks interesting to them. Provide a thinksheet that requires short snippets of writing—like the double-entry diary. Don't focus on the amount of spaces filled. Focus on the quality of thinking. Challenge students who have nothing written to get one piece of thinking down. Respond to that one piece of thinking and then challenge them to go for two thoughts the following day. Success breeds success! When conferring, model again how to use the thinksheet. Maybe offer to do the reading and then be their secretary by writing down their thinking. Stress that they don't have to write a lot to show that they are interacting with text. A little is better than nothing.

4. **What do I do when kids don't care enough about their work to revise.** Sometimes students don't revise because they see no purpose in doing so. Other times students don't revise because they don't know how. Many confuse revision with editing. Thinksheets collect thinking over time so kids can see how they are getting smarter. When students use their thinksheets as scaffolds to help them write or create a more sophisticated piece of work, they are more willing to re-enter the revision process. It's also important to remember that students don't want to revise when they don't get feedback along the way. Without feedback, it's hard to know how to change original drafts.

5. **What do I do if kids can't read grade-level material?** For starters, find them another text! The only way students will get better at reading is to read. If they fake read all period,

it's just a waste of time. Thinksheets also tell students that meaning doesn't "arrive" but has to be constructed. They help students monitor their thinking and repair meaning. They also help teachers see what striving readers need so the teacher can provide support. Thinksheets help students experiment with different ways to construct meaning.

6. **What do I do with students who don't care or aren't moti-vated to do anything?** Provide choice and a platform to actually use the information. Don't focus on the amount of thinking held, focus on quality. Today, students may only get one box or line completed. Tomorrow, they might be moti-vated to go for two. Responding to students in a couple of places shows them that you care about their learning lives. If you can, share with the class a line of smart thinking that an unmotivated student has written. It reassures the reluctant or unconfident student that they are on the right track. Using something from the previous day's work to adjust instruc-tion tells them that you are paying careful attention to their learning needs.

Thinksheets aren't a magic bullet. But they do help us know each student better—as a person and as a learner. They take the focus off of the "one right answer" and allow learners to enter into the process wherever they are. Thinksheets let students surprise us with their thinking. They fill up our head and heart with connections that matter, so we can tend to learners with future texts and tasks and tend to their needs. Thinksheets demonstrate to students that their thinking and growth matter most.

What Works? Five CYA Structures That Help Students Remove the Masks of Invisibility

1. Use thinksheets to assess if students care about the **Topic**. If they don't, share a few compelling reasons either through **Texts**, case studies, or questions about why the **Topic** matters. This will increase emotional and cognitive engagement.

2. Use thinksheets to assess and adjust the **Text, Target, Task,** and **Time** for the students who are disengaging. Maybe you will need to find a different **Text** for a student or shift a **Target**. Sometimes the **Task** has to be broken down into smaller steps. Consider if the student may just need more **Time**.

3. Use the thinksheets to give a little bit of attention to everyone. If time is short, **Tend** to students' thinksheets that you didn't confer with during class. A comment or two on each sheet will show students' that you care about their thinking even when you didn't talk to them in class. Reading thinksheets will also help you notice patterns that will steer student learning toward hitting whatever standard they are going for.

4. Do your own assignment. Then you can use your thinksheet as a model. When you do this, you send the message that the **Task** is worthy of students' **Time**.

5. Respond directly on the thinksheets. Share how thinksheets help you to adjust students' **Texts, Targets,** and **Tasks** the next day. Emphasize that their thinking matters more than a right answer when it comes to you **Tend**ing to their needs.

Chapter 7

When You Care, You Fall More

Growing up in Colorado, I started skiing when I was very young. If you saw me ski today, you'd probably think to yourself, *Wow, she's skied her whole life? You'd think she'd be a lot better.* There was a reason I didn't improve. I hated taking risks because they usually ended up in a fall. Not only did falls hurt, but they were scary. Unfortunately for me, my family viewed wiping out on steeper and harder slopes as a badge of honor.

After a long day of skiing, on the drive home, the first question my dad would ask each of us was, "How many times did you fall today?"

My oldest brother, Mark, the best skier in the family, always fell the most. "At *least* twelve times!" he'd brag. Mark pushed himself to try new techniques and ski bigger moguls, and because of this, he never stopped getting better. My dad would praise him and make him the example. "Do you know why Mark is such a good skier?" he'd ask rhetorically. "It's because he isn't afraid to fall."

I'd hear these words and roll my eyes. *Twelve times,* I'd think, *Geez, I haven't fallen twelve times in my entire life.* As each brother reported his number, I braced for my turn and the usual outcry from the car. When Dad asked, "Cris, what's your number?", my response was always the same. "Zero."

That was the cue for everyone in the car to chime in, even my mom! (Although to be honest, she used a different motivational tactic.) "You know, Cris, if you don't learn how to ski well by the time you get to high school, you won't be invited on ski trips. What if you like a boy who is a good skier? When he finds out you can't keep up with him, he'll invite someone else."

No matter what carrot was dangled, my dedication to safety reigned supreme over my dedication to improving. Their nagging only made me more resolute to stay on top of my skis. I was good enough. I didn't care enough to risk falling more.

Teaching students is a lot more complex than skiing moguls. To serve them well, I have to work to continually grow my skills as a teacher. This is something I care about deeply, and I know that if I don't stumble and fall, I won't get better. For the students who need me the most, I can't take it safe and slow. I have to wipe out to get better. Frequently, my risks take place during demonstration lessons, in classrooms where I don't know the kids, or the content. This vulnerability—trying something new in front of others, forces me to walk the talk of what I ask teachers to do. Try something new and risk a spectacular fail.

The first day of trying anything new is always hard. Students may be leery of the changes we make and they may go to great lengths to protect themselves from embarrassment. I get it. I think a lot of teachers are like that too. But it's hard to improve our craft if there isn't vulnerability coursing through the classroom. Failing doesn't feel good, but sometimes it's where we learn our best lessons.

Teachers Wear Masks, Too

Frequently during professional development days, I work to help secondary science and social studies teachers appreciate how students feel when they are assigned to read complex scientific and historical text. Secondary teachers know their content well and have read their required material often. Some may have forgotten what it feels like to read sophisticated content for the first time.

To help teachers remember this "first time feeling," I ask them to read something complex and out of their comfort zone. Recently, I asked teachers to read the twenty-third chapter of *Moby Dick*, "The Lee Shore" (Melville 1851). The chapter is short. It's so short, that in some literary circles it is referred to as the "six-inch" chapter. Some experts argue that Melville wrote it to tout his views on existentialism—that it is best to live life to its fullest because death is imminent. The character in this chapter is a sailor named Bulkington, who decides to leave the safety of the shore to sail the stormy seas. He perishes doing what he loves. Bulkington is eulogized for taking risks to live his life to the fullest, even though his "living" causes him to die. Apparently, to Melville, it was better to die doing what you love than to live a life of boredom, staying safely on the shore.

Without context or Sparknotes, the chapter is almost impossible to make sense of. I observe teachers as they read. Quite quickly after beginning the section, they get off task. There is nothing funny about the chapter, yet quiet giggles erupt from different parts of the room. Often a teacher will lean over to another and crack a joke. The listening teacher stops reading and laughs at the comment. When I ask, "What's so funny?" it never has anything to do with the task at hand. Like students who struggle, teachers also have ways to avoid "not knowing."

Other teachers sit on the sidelines or get up and leave the room when asked to read. Sometimes they will pull out papers to grade, so when I ask to hear what they think about the piece, they can deflect or admit that they didn't actually read it. Better to put on the mask of apathy than to be wrong. Right?

I'm convinced that we all wear masks as defense mechanisms. It's a way for learners to protect themselves from being vulnerable or unprepared. When learners don't get approval for achieving in the way the person in charge expects, they seek approval elsewhere or don the mask of invisibility to take the heat off their performance.

A Last Look at Our Big Questions

I tweaked our frequently asked questions one last time, to drive teacher agency and efficacy:

- How do I structure **Time, Text, Tasks, and Targets** every day and over time so each student has agency to think for themselves?

- How might I **Tend** to each student to help them find connections so they care about their learning? Who needs tending most?

- Which **Texts** might provide each student with entry points for background knowledge, or a model of craft, so no one refuses to read and write?

- What authentic **Task** might I ask each kid to care enough about to revise over **Time**?

- What variety of **Texts** might help each kid eventually read grade-level material over time?

- What **Topics** do I harness to help each student to care and motivate all students to be critical thinkers, world-focused citizens, and problem solvers?

Don't let the questions psych you out. It's not a to-do list or a mandate, but rather a way to think about hooking our most challenging kids. The best teachers strive to engage all students. This is admirable and sometimes aggravating. If you're like me, you sometimes obsess over the ones who aren't doing what we want and this gets discouraging. When I get into this rut, I take some time to reflect on the good work that is happening in the classroom. When teachers give themselves credit for all of the students whose needs are being met, it's easier to re-enter the teaching and learning process to figure out another way to reach the mask-wearers who drive us nuts.

For example, instead of thinking about what disengaged kids can't do, try thinking about what they *could* do if we tried something different. Instead of feeling like a kid just doesn't care, assume positive intent, and trust that they could be successful if they were provided with a different text, task, or target.

Years ago, a student named Mallorie helped me to figure out that disengaged students wear masks to play a role and that these masks aren't necessarily who they are or want to be. Last fall, out of the blue, this former student found me on Facebook. There are so many reasons to detest this platform. Perhaps its only redeeming quality is that it helps people reconnect, and that's what Mallorie did. She reached out to ask my advice.

> Hey Ms. Tovani! Hope things are well with you. I just had my son's parent-teacher conferences and he is struggling with comprehending nonfiction and I was wondering if you had any tips that I can do at home to get him on track?

> Hi Mallorie, you're such a good mom. Read nonfiction to him—whatever he likes. Pause a few times and ask him what he's thinking. Remember that inner voice stuff? The waste of time voice is when your mind wanders as you read. Show him the conversation voice that talks back to the text. You can talk to the text by asking questions, making connections, giving an opinion, inferring… BTW how old is your son?

He is almost eleven and is on grade level for comprehending fiction but for some reason, he is way behind when it comes to comprehending nonfiction.

He probably got bored with the nonfiction reading passages on the test and maybe his mind wandered. What if you help him notice how nonfiction is different from fiction? I bet that will help.

I will give it a try. Thanks Ms. Tovani.

You bet. It was great to hear from you.

Good to hear from you too. I have five kids and only three are in school so I'm sure I will need more of your advice down the road. Lol.

Five kids! Wow! It's hard to image that this sweet Facebook exchange came from Mallorie. It's been at least twenty years since I taught her, but I clearly remember this former ninth grader who wore every mask available to keep her teachers at a distance. At the beginning of the year, I was sure she didn't care about learning to read better or even about school, for that matter. Now, she's tracked me down on Facebook to get advice for her kids.

I was curious, so I did a little digging in some dusty boxes in my basement and found Mallorie's conversation calendar from the first week of school. I was sure I had saved it because what she wrote was so different from what she projected. At the time, Mallorie was going through her goth stage. She dressed in black, and her light skin magnified the dark lipstick she wore. As I read her Monday entry, I remember Mallorie's mask of anger. That first day of school, her eyes glared and dared me to engage her. Surprisingly though, on her portion of Monday's conversation calendar, she tells me that over the weekend she went mountain biking and wiped out. She thinks she cracked a rib. I try to picture the kid in the room riding a bike. As a sidenote, she gives me the heads-up that she doesn't like to smile or talk.

The following day, Mallorie shows up wearing the mask of apathy, her head on the desk, propped up on her arm just enough for me to see her eye-rolling. Yet on today's conversation calendar, she writes that she likes Italian. Her seemingly out of context comment confuses me. At first, I think she is telling me that she likes my last name. Then I realize she is referring to the short piece of text "Di Tri Berrese" (Source Unknown). I had students read it that day to help them see that they had to do more than sound out words to make meaning.

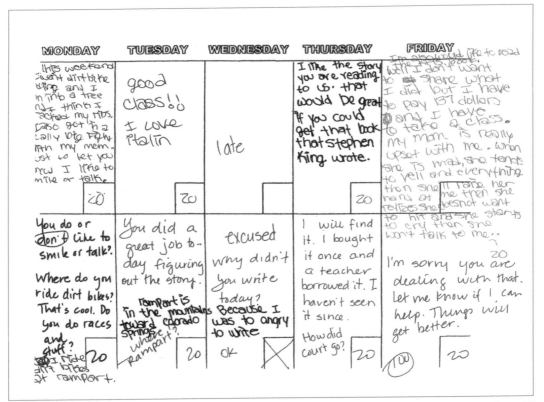

Figure 7.1
Mallorie's Conversation Calendar

Wednesday, Mallorie is late to class, the mask of anger is back on, and she doesn't write on her calendar. Thursday, she seems lighter, even class-clownish. On my portion of the calendar, Mallorie writes that she was too angry to write on Wednesday, but today she asks if I can get her a Stephen King book. Excitedly, I tell her, "Yes!" Later that afternoon, I run into Mallorie's dean and learn that a court appearance was the cause for Wednesday's tardiness. So, on her calendar, I write, "How did court go?"

Mallorie's Friday response takes me aback. She writes, "Well, I don't want to share what I did, but I have to pay $137.00 and I have to take a class. My mom is really upset with me. When she is mad she tends to yell and everything. Then she'll raise her hand at me, then she realizes that she doesn't want to hit and she starts to cry and then she won't talk to me." The saddest part of the whole response for me is the sad face emoji she draws at the bottom. The conversation calendar gave me insight into the mask Mallorie wore. I realized that her life outside of school was perhaps complicating her life inside of school. But this didn't mean that she didn't care about learning, literacy, or getting smarter. Again and again, I'm reminded that making assumptions about kids' appearances and attitudes gets us into trouble when we don't take time to know them as people.

The Six Ts Are Our Tools

Like so many of our challenging kids, Mallorie did her best to prove to me that she was unteachable. Sometimes students' masks can fool us into thinking that they just don't want to learn. But no one wants to fail. People don't start their day hoping to be embarrassed and disenfranchised. As human beings, we are wired to learn. Knowing ways to help students take off their masks keeps us from giving up on them. Harnessing the Six Ts gives teachers different entry points for reaching students who seemingly don't want to engage.

For example, using the **Tend to Me** and **Text** Ts helps me to connect to students who come to class angry. By making a connection with students, I can often remove the mask of anger with a kind word, a book recommendation, or an introduction to another student.

Utilizing **Targets** and **Tasks** does wonders for the students wearing the mask of class clown because it gives them authentic purposes and audiences with whom to share their work. They see a clear learning goal and know that they don't have to perform for the class to get attention. They have a real audience who will see the fruits of their labor.

Arming myself with the minilesson connected to **Tasks** that come from students' needs, I can hook the kids wearing the masks of apathy, invisibility, and minimal effort. They no longer have to act like they don't care or try to disappear. Showing students how to hit the targets using models, each other, and me helps them access content. When I adjust my instruction and give them feedback based on their work, they know I'm paying careful attention to their thinking.

By focusing my planning around the Ts of **Topic** and **Time,** I can anticipate for any mask that shows up. Nesting skills into a compelling topic—and being realistic about the time it will take to produce quality work—tells each student that this isn't going to be a one-and-done kind of class.

Creating an environment where students engage for the majority of minutes requires planning and flexibility. Great teachers are a lot like mixed martial arts fighters. They don't handcuff themselves to one philosophy or technique. Like MMA fighters, they strategize and use moves from all different experts. Excellent teachers, like MMA fighters, adjust their methods and strategies to meet the needs of students. They modify their planning and instruction to meet the demands of the situation. Great teachers anticipate the students they will have. They gather tools they might need and plan different ways to keep students engaged. Anticipating what students might need before they even enter the room keeps me from getting teaching battle scars.

Below is one of the charts I use to think about my future students. It helps me consider what to prepare for so that more students are engaged.

Anticipating What Students Might Need

Kinds of Learners I Anticipate	Questions to Ponder	What Might Each Learner Need to Engage?	Example of Text, Task, Target, Tend to Me
Students who act out to avoid learning			
Students who act overconfident or project an air of knowing it all and claim boredom			
Students who comply to get through the assignment			
Striving readers/learners			
Non-native English speakers			
Students who are tired, hungry, in need of nurturing			
Excelling, eager, unchallenged learners			

Anticipating What Students Might Need *Example*

Kinds of Learners I Anticipate	Questions to Ponder	What Might Each Learner Need to Engage?	Example of Text, Task, Target, Tend to Me
Students who act out to avoid learning	What is blocking their willingness to engage? What roadblocks can I remove? What might they need right now to engage?	Personal attention Connection to something they care about	**Text:** Find a short, engaging text from a newspaper, magazine, or picture book that might be intriguing.
Students who act overconfident or project an air of knowing it all and claim boredom	Are they hiding a deficit? Are they afraid to fail? Do they have a fixed mindset? Are they really bored?	An opportunity to demonstrate what they do know Reassurance that smart people admit confusion and work to clear it	**Target:** I can demonstrate what I already know and what I need to know next about the topic.
Students who comply to get through the assignment	Is the purpose clear to learners? Are the text, task, and target worthy of their time?	Examples of how the work they are doing will pay off Examples of where the work resides in the world	**Task:** Provide students with an authentic audience for the task.
Striving readers/learners	Can they decode? Do they know how to recognize when they are stuck? Do they have ways to talk back to text?	Thinking strategies to talk back to text Success reading a piece of text they care about	**Text:** Lots of short text that is engaging (lyrics, poems, infographics, graphic novels)
Non-native English speakers	Can they read in their first language? Where can I find text in their native language?	A partner to work with Text in the native language next to the English version	**Text:** Lots of short text that is engaging (lyrics, poems, infographics, graphic novels)
Students who are tired, hungry, in need of nurturing	What do they need most right now? Can I connect them to a service that will provide for basic needs?	A breakfast bar, a place to sleep, a safe person to talk to	**Tend:** Some personal attention to build trust and assess physical and SEL needs.
Excelling, eager, unchallenged learners	What makes these students tick? What are they curious about? What is novel or new that might push or entice them to dig into the work?	Choice Sophisticated models	**Text:** that challenges **Topic:** that is unfamiliar **Tasks:** that are complex

One Last Story

Sometimes students are bored for good reason. Recently, I was working in a district that believed that testing kids every six weeks would not only measure progress, but would improve it. The testing took time away from instruction and practice. In one particular building where I was asked to do some demonstration teaching, test scores were exceptionally low. Students and teachers alike were demoralized.

As I walked through the halls, I was struck by how grey everything seemed. The walls were blank, the teachers' affect was blank, and worst of all, students seemed despondent. It was clear that teaching to the test was the captor in chief.

After the second day of morning demonstration lessons and afternoon teacher learning, I reflected on the bright spots of learning that had happened. I was sure the second-day teachers had noticed them too. Unfortunately, there was still little energy after the demo. I felt like I had done everything I could to model different ways that teachers could increase student engagement. But at every turn, I heard teachers say, "These kids are really low," "They don't care about school," "They can't read or write," "They just don't care." By the afternoon debrief, I had had it!

Then, Dickie (yes, that really was his name), a seventh-grade science teacher, spoke up. He was in a full-on rant about his students and mid-complaint, I held my hand up and said, "Stop. Let's think about this for a minute. Our job is to teach students about content that we love so much that we have dedicated our lives to teaching it."

The room got quiet. Then Dickie defiantly barked, "Kids have changed. They don't care about school or science or reading or writing. Some can't even speak English."

I paused, knowing that what I said next would either alienate or support these very frustrated teachers. I look back at my response with regret that I didn't have the courage to call out Dickie's racist remarks. Instead, I acknowledged the crushing pressure of testing, I said, "I know that all of this assessing is tough and when kids don't show growth on their results, it's discouraging. When I feel discouraged because kids aren't doing what I want them to do, I have to ask myself three questions." In my best Clint Eastwood imitation, I paused for effect: "I ask myself: 'Is my content boring? Is my lesson boring? Or am I boring?'"

The room grew quiet. Looking directly at him, I ask, "Dickie, do you think your content is boring?"

With a quick no, he says, "Physical science is amazing."

I nod my head. "Well then, is the lesson or unit you are teaching boring?"

After a few seconds of thought, Dickie says, "Well, Newton's laws aren't that fun for middle schoolers to learn but once you learn them, you can explain why a soccer ball angles the way it does or why concussions are such a problem when kids collide. Students need to learn the facts before they can figure out how things work."

I nod my head, not because I thought that kids needed all the facts first, but because he did seem to care about and have some real-world connections to his content. I ask the final question, "Well then, are you boring?"

Without responding, Dickie stomped out of the room. Clearly, he had had it with me, and frankly I was tired of him too. He gave up on our professional development cohort. Sadly, I wondered if he also gave up on his students, or if my comment stuck in his craw, and nudged him to take some risks to structure lessons using the physics of sport to engage more kids. Blaming kids is never OK. If I could do it over again, I would have addressed his racist comment and reminded him that our job is to figure out why our content is worthy of all students. I let the assessment take the fall for Dickie's unwillingness to tend to all students by differentiating time, texts, tasks, and targets.

We Determine the Weather

I get it. We've all been frustrated when we can't get kids to do what we want. But we determine the weather as chief learners in the classroom. We have a choice. We can stormily enter the room and with a grumpy face look at our students with disappointment and disdain. Or, we can be a ray of light and come to class giving and expecting the best. We can blindly follow a curriculum guide that someone else has made, or we can use it to enhance our own long-term planning to ensure that our content is compelling, accessible, and reflective of all learners. It's up to us. We decide who we give up on and who we try to re-engage. We hold a lot of power.

I came across a quote from American psychologist Jerome Bruner. It read, "We teach who we are." Are you the kind of teacher who believes that each kid can learn if we create the conditions? Are you the kind of teacher who is relentless in finding ways to help students re-engage? Are you the kind of teacher who wants to make a difference? If you've made it this far, you are probably all three.

I'm guessing that you not only love your subject matter, but you also love kids. So, what risk will you take to plan differently for your students? How will you work to make your unit more compelling? How will you align the targets to tasks? When will you make time to find different texts so that all students can access and see themselves reflected in the content? Will you plan to spend a little time each day to connect and show tenderness to a student who probably needs it more than you know? There are so many choices we can make to re-engage students. It's up to you, because not only are you the heat, cold, wind, and rain—you're also the sun—which all living things need to grow and flourish.

Appendices

Appendix A: Learning Target Rubrics

- Book Review Learning Target Rubric
- Dream Speech Learning Target Rubric
- Infographic Learning Target Rubric
- Open Letter Learning Target Rubric
- Sample Learning Target Rubrics

Appendix B: Double-Entry Diaries

- Generic Double-Entry Diary
- Double-Entry Diary: Nonfiction
- Double-Entry Diary: Fiction
- Double-Entry Diary: Science
- Double-Entry Diary: Social Studies
- Double-Entry Diary: WWII Annotated Version

Appendix C: Inner Voice Sheets

- Generic Inner Voice Sheet
- Inner Voice Sheet: *Of Mice and Men* Example
- Inner Voice Sheet: Social Studies/Science
- Inner Voice Sheet: Math

Appendix D: Synthesis Sheets

- Generic Synthesis Sheet
- Synthesis Thinksheet: Theme Example
- Synthesis Thinksheet: Science
- Synthesis Thinksheet: Kinetic Energy
- Synthesis Thinksheet: Kinetic Energy Example

Appendix E: Vocabulary Builder

- Vocabulary Builder Thinksheet
- Vocabulary Builder Annotated Thinksheet: Force and Motion
- Connect Two

Appendix F: Silent Reading Response Sheet

Appendix G: Virtual Background Knowledge Placemats

Annotated Book Review Learning Target Rubric

Annotated book reviews are short and help readers decide if a book is worthy of their money and time. They give readers an idea of what the book is about but don't share everything. They tantalize readers with juicy snippets that encourage them to read more. Your challenge is to create an annotated book review to share with other students that will encourage them to read during their free time.

Name:

Final Annotated Book Review Due:

Editing as a Courtesy to the Reader:

Student Reflection	Teacher Reflection	Learning Targets
_____	_____	**5 points:** I can capitalize, punctuate, and spell correctly as a courtesy to readers.
_____	_____	**5 points:** I can include the following information to help readers locate the book: title, author, copyright information, publisher, and length.
_____	_____	**5 points:** I can embed a visual representation of the cover as a reference for potential readers.
_____	_____	**5 points:** I can demonstrate improvement by attaching drafts.

Thinking Behind the Annotated Book Review:

Student Reflection	Teacher Reflection	Learning Targets
_____	_____	**5 points:** I can write a powerful first sentence to grab readers' attention.
_____	_____	**10 points:** I can give readers a basic idea of what the book is about without spoiling the end.
_____	_____	**5 points:** I can rate the book using a five-star rating system and recommend a specific age group or population who might enjoy the book.
_____	_____	**10 points:** I can describe why readers should read the book.

Student total: _____ out of 50 points　**Teacher total:** _____ out of 50 points

Here's what I want you to know about my process:

Dream Speech Learning Target Rubric

Well-written and delivered speeches move people to action. Your challenge is to deliver a speech that creates awareness about a topic and encourages the people who hear you to do something. Your speech will be written and delivered to an audience of your choosing.

Name:

Final Written Speech Due:

Delivered Speech Given By:

Student Reflection	Teacher Reflection	Learning Targets
——————	——————	**10 points:** I can capitalize, punctuate, and spell correctly as a courtesy to readers.
——————	——————	**10 points:** I can begin my speech with an interesting opening line, story, joke, or question.
——————	——————	**10 points:** I can describe why the audience should care about my topic.
——————	——————	**10 points:** I can incorporate two of the following rhetorical devices to gain my audience's trust: ethos, logos, or pathos.
——————	——————	**10 points:** I can emphasize a point by repeating a key phrase or line at least three times throughout the speech.
——————	——————	**10 points:** I can call my readers to action by asking them to do something in support of my topic.
——————	——————	**10 points:** I can demonstrate improvement by attaching drafts.

Delivered Speech
Audience members will evaluate you on the following:

Student Reflection	Teacher Reflection	Learning Targets
——————	——————	**10 points:** I can deliver my speech only periodically looking at my notes.
——————	——————	**10 points:** I can vary the tone of my voice.
——————	——————	**10 points:** I can speak so that my audience understands me.

Student total: —————— **out of 100 points**   **Teacher total:** —————— **out of 100 points**

Here's what I want you to know about my process:

Infographic Learning Target Rubric

Infographics organize a variety of visual images that convey information. Your challenge is to create an infographic that synthesizes and shares new learning. You will provide readers with multiple entry points into the topic and design your infographic so that it is pleasing to the eye.

Name:

Final Infographic Due:

Editing as a Courtesy to the Reader:

Student Reflection	Teacher Reflection	Learning Targets
_____	_____	**10 points:** I can capitalize, punctuate, and spell correctly as a courtesy to readers.
_____	_____	**10 points:** I can design my infographic using color and strategic placement of items.
_____	_____	**10 points:** I can cite credible sources correctly and give credit to the original thinker.
_____	_____	**10 points:** I can demonstrate design improvements by attaching drafts.

Thinking Behind the Infographic:

Student Reflection	Teacher Reflection	Learning Targets
_____	_____	**10 points:** I can design my infographic around an issue or a specific topic.
_____	_____	**10 points:** I can provide information that shares different points of view.
_____	_____	**10 points:** I can embed statistics.
_____	_____	**10 points:** I can share compelling photos that haven't been doctored.
_____	_____	**10 points:** I can create curiosity about the topic so that people want to know more.

Student total: _____ **out of 90 points**   **Teacher total:** _____ **out of 90 points**

Here's what I want you to know about my process:

Open Letter Learning Target Rubric

Typically an open letter is addressed to a well-known person or community but is intended for a wider audience. Your open letter challenge is to create awareness about a sensitive issue connected to _____. Using political and social upheaval examples, current events, and stories, write an open letter to someone who needs to hear your argument. Be sure to use evidence to support your position.

Name:

Final Open Letter Due:

Editing as a Courtesy to the Reader:

Student Reflection	Teacher Reflection	Learning Targets
_____	_____	**10 points:** I can capitalize, punctuate, and spell correctly as a courtesy to readers.
_____	_____	**10 points:** I can embed quotes correctly so I don't interrupt the flow of my message.
_____	_____	**10 points:** I can cite sources correctly to credit the original thinker.
_____	_____	**10 points:** I can demonstrate improvement by attaching drafts.

Thinking Behind the Open Letter:

Student Reflection	Teacher Reflection	Learning Targets
_____	_____	**10 points:** I can describe an issue surrounding the current Syrian refugee crisis.
_____	_____	**10 points:** I can take a position on the current Syrian refugee crisis argument.
_____	_____	**10 points:** I can embed a statistic and a fact to support my position.
_____	_____	**10 points:** I can share a short narrative that illustrates how people connected to this crisis are affected.
_____	_____	**10 points:** I can call readers to action by asking them to do something that will create awareness about the Syrian refugee crisis.

Student total: _____ out of 90 points   **Teacher total:** _____ out of 90 points

Here's what I want you to know about my process:

Sample Learning Targets that Grow Readers and Writers over Time (in alphabetical order by VERB)

- I can **analyze** data to predict future trends.

- I can **analyze** what an author has a character say and do to infer who they are.

- I can **articulate** how the author structures the text to help me understand the story.

- I can **ask** questions and make connections to help me start reading a book.

- I can **ask** questions I care about to sustain my reading.

- I can **ask** questions to isolate confusion.

- I can **ask** questions as I read to know what background knowledge I need next to build understanding.

- I can **build** background knowledge for a novel by reading nonfiction.

- I can **combine** textual evidence with my background knowledge to infer meaning.

- I can **connect** to something I know to help me understand something new.

- I can **describe** how factual information connects to a topic.

- I can **determine** importance by setting a purpose for my reading.

- I can **go** beyond the graphics and words to infer meaning.

- I can **hold** my thinking about my reading in an organized fashion so that it is useful when it's time to discuss or write.

- I can **identify** unknown words and decide which ones are most important to learn.

- I can **manipulate** my inner voice to help me re-enter the text when I'm confused.

- I can **monitor** my understanding so that I am able to recognize and repair my confusion.

- I can **organize** my background knowledge into an infographic to help a reader learn a new concept or idea.

- I can **recognize** when my inner voice is wandering.

- I can **reread** confusing parts differently.

- I can **sift** and **sort** the nonfiction I read based on my purpose.

- I can **synthesize** information from multiple texts to show new thinking.

- I can **use** nonfiction text structures to guide me to the information that I need to read.

- I can **use** the first-hand experience of an author to inform my argument.

- I can **use** a mentor text to inspire and influence my writing.

- I can **use** the thinking I've held on my reading to begin crafting a piece of writing.

- I can **visualize** something I know to help me make a picture in my mind when I read.

For more information on learning targets and how I use them to support learning over time, see *So What Do They Really Know? Assessment That Informs Teaching and Learning* (2010).

Double-Entry Diary

Topic:

Daily/Weekly Learning Targets:

Record a new fact or a piece of information that you find interesting. (Don't forget to record your source and page number so that you can refer back to it.)	SO WHAT? Why does the information matter? What struck you about the fact you wrote? If you are confused or curious, ask a question. If it connects to something you already know, write the connection and why it matters.
1.	1.
2.	2.
3.	3.
4.	4.
5.	5.

Here's how I got smarter about today's topic and targets:

ENGLISH/LANGUAGE ARTS:
Nonfiction Text Selections for the novel *Night* by Elie Wiesel (1982)

Daily/Weekly Learning Targets:

- I can monitor and manipulate my inner voice to talk back to the text.
- I can build my background knowledge about a historical time period to help me understand how setting drives plot.

Line from the text that builds my background knowledge or causes me to think in a new way:	Connection to history, current event, or human nature, Question about something in the text or something about human nature that is confusing, or New Thinking for Me:
1.	1.
2.	2.

Here's what I've figured out and wonder about the novel *Night*:

ENGLISH/LANGUAGE ARTS:
Night by Elie Wiesel

Daily/Weekly Supporting Targets:

- I can monitor and manipulate my inner voice to talk back to the text.
- I can share questions and new thinking with my book club to grow my understanding of a literary work.

Line and page number from the text that I want to share:	Questions about something in the text or New Thinking for Me:
1.	1.
2.	2.

Here's what I've figured out and wonder about the novel *Night*:

Environmental SCIENCE:
Population Pyramids and Demographic Data

Daily/Weekly Supporting Targets:

- I can predict future trends by analyzing historical data.
- I can ask questions to isolate my confusion.

What Do I Observe? Describe what you observe in the data, graph, or table.	**What Does It Mean?** Record any questions, predictions, or hypotheses you have connected to your observation.
1.	1.
2.	2.

What future population trends can you infer based on the historical data? Reflect on the learning targets. What do you need next?

SOCIAL STUDIES:
World War II European Theater

Daily/Weekly Supporting Targets:

- I can build background knowledge about historical events to better help me understand the present.
- I can articulate why the information I am sharing matters.

Record a fact or a piece of information that interests you.	SO WHAT? How does this fact/information help you understand today? Why does this fact/information matter? What questions do you have about this fact/information?
1.	1.
2.	2.

Here's how I got smarter about today's learning targets and WWII:

World War II-The European Theater

Daily/Weekly Learning Targets:
- I can read to build my background knowledge about WWII so that I have a better understanding of its causes and effects on today.
- I can articulate why the information I share is important.

These targets change based on students' needs and the teacher's long-term learning targets.

Usually all students need to record in this column is a line or two to help them remember the words that caused the thinking.

This is the matched assessment to the targets. In this column, students demonstrate how they are approaching or hitting the targets.

Record a new fact or a piece of information that you find interesting. (Don't forget to record your source and page number so that you can refer back to it.)	SO WHAT? Why does the information matter? What struck you about the fact you wrote? If you are confused or curious, ask a question. If it connects to something you already know, write the connection and why it matters.
1. *This column also grounds the reader so the adjacent column makes sense.*	1. *The options can vary based on what the teacher's learning targets are and what she wants student to demon-strate.*
2.	2. *I wanted students to show me that they could do more than copy facts. I wanted them to articulate why the facts matter and how they connect*
3.	3. *to a bigger understanding of history.*
4.	4.
5.	5.

Here's how I got smarter about today's topic and targets: *Below, I want students to reflect and synthesize new thinking. Sometimes this writing help them see bigger ideas and it help me to see what they know and need.*

Inner Voice Sheet

Begin reading on page _____. Record the conversation you have in your head as you read. If you catch your mind wandering as you read, give yourself a job of something to pay attention to. See if you can **ask a question** to isolate a confusion or if you can **make a connection** to something you know to draw an inference. If you read something that you think is important but aren't sure why, **record the quote** and see if you can take a stab at **what it means to you**.

Inner voice on page:	Inner voice on page:

Inner voice on page:	Inner voice on page:

ENGLISH/LANGUAGE ARTS/FREE CHOICE/ CLASS NOVEL:
Inner Voice Sheet: *Of Mice and Men* by John Steinbeck

Begin reading on page _____. Record the conversation you are having in your head as you read. If you catch your mind wandering as you read, assign yourself something to pay attention to. Reread that chunk with a purpose. For example: **Ask a question to isolate a confusion. Make a connection to something you know. Infer a character's actions** by thinking about how you'd respond in that situation. If you read something that you think is important but aren't sure why, **record the sentence and see if you can take a stab at what you think it means to you.**

Inner Voice on page:	Inner Voice on page:
Inner Voice on page:	Inner Voice on page:

SOCIAL STUDIES/SCIENCE:
Inner Voice Sheet: Recipe for Revolution

Record the conversation you have in your head as you read the informational text you've selected. If you catch your mind wandering as you read, assign yourself something to pay attention to. See if you can **ask a question** to isolate a confusion or **paraphrase something** that you've read. If you read something that you think is important but aren't sure why, record the words and see if you can **take a stab at what it means to you**.

King George, Lobsterbacks, and Loyalists	Founding Fathers, Firebrands, and Patriots
Taxes, Trouble, and the Tea Party	Ideals, Declarations, and Propaganda

MATHEMATICAL:
Inner Voice Sheet

Possible ways to record mathematical thinking using pictures, numbers, and/or words:

- Identify skills or processes needed to solve the problem.
- Record what is known about solving the problem.
- Show calculations.
- List questions to isolate confusion.
- Explain why the solution is reasonable and valid.
- Draw a picture or diagram.

As you read the problem, where do you start? What do you know that might help you with this problem?	What questions emerge as you work the problem? Isolate any confusion by asking a question.
Show your steps as you work the problem. Pay attention to your "inner voice" that is saying, "First I should . . . then I should . . ."	Based on the steps you took, explain why your answer is reasonable and valid.

Synthesis Sheet

Synthesis Sheet for:

Literary Element Study of:

Weekly/Daily Learning Targets:

Here's what I remember reading:

Here's what I wonder:

When I study _____, I pay attention to:

I also notice:

Synthesis Sheet for *Theme*

Here's what I remember reading:

Here's what I'm wondering:

I noticed some possible motifs (**recurrent** patterns, ideas, images, objects, and symbols) that help readers develop a theme. Motifs are written in **one or two words.**

Here is a motif written as a theme statement:

Science Synthesis Thinksheet

Daily/Weekly Learning Targets:

Science vocabulary that I might need:

This is my claim (how I think _____ works):

Study the model of the _____ and observe _____ at the beginning, middle, and end. Hypothesize what you think is happening:

Beginning	Middle	End
First attempt:	First attempt:	First attempt:
After some science reading, now I think:	After some science reading, now I think:	After some science reading, now I think:

Using the scientific vocabulary for the unit, write your explanation how

_____ :

Kinetic Energy Synthesis Thinksheet

What? Roller Coasters Don't Have Engines!
Daily/Weekly Learning Targets:

- I can describe how data changes over time.
- I can use vocabulary connected to kinetic energy to explain what I observe.
- I can describe how energy changes to explain how roller coasters move.

Science vocabulary that I might need:

This is my claim (how I think roller coasters work):

Study the paper model of the roller coaster and observe its movement at the beginning, middle, and end. Hypothesize what you think is happening:

Beginning	Middle	End
First attempt:	First attempt:	First attempt:
After some science reading, now I think:	After some science reading, now I think:	After some science reading, now I think:

Using the following vocabulary stems, write your explanation describing how roller coasters move:

- Potential energy increases/decreases as...
- Kinetic energy increases/decreases as...
- Speed increases/decreases as...
- Friction causes the cars to _____ as _____

Kinetic Energy Synthesis Thinksheet

What? Roller Coasters Don't Have Engines! *Example*

Daily/Weekly Learning Targets:

- I can describe how data changes over time.
- I can use vocabulary connected to kinetic energy to explain what I observe.
- I can describe how energy changes to explain how rollercoasters move.

Science vocabulary that I might need:

height, mass, force, acceleration, gravity, friction

This is my claim (how I think) roller coasters work:

I have no idea. I thought roller coasters had engines. I think that gravity might have something to do with their movement at the top of the hill, but I wonder how cars get to the top of the hill.

Study the paper model of the roller coaster and observe its movement at the beginning, middle, and end. Hypothesize what you think is happening:

Beginning	Middle	End
First attempt:	First attempt:	First attempt:
The higher the hill greater the incline, the slower the speed. (This might be something I need to add to my claim.)	*Maybe the mass of the cars causes it to go faster accelerate.*	*Something keeps the cars on the track. It's a force of some kind. I'm going to read for different kinds of forces.*
After some science reading, now I think:	After some science reading, now I think:	After some science reading, now I think:
Friction causes the cars to slow. *Potential energy increases as the cars climb. (I looked at the stems below to use scientific vocabulary.)*	*Is gravity a force pulling the cars? Does this increase the speed?*	

Using the following vocabulary stems, write your explanation describing how roller coasters move:

- Potential energy increases/decreases as...
- Kinetic energy increases/decreases as...
- Speed increases/decreases as...
- Friction causes the cars to _____ as _____

Vocabulary Builders Thinksheet

Learning Target(s):

Word Bank Possibilities:

New Vocabulary	What I Think I Know	Diagram/Example	What I Wonder

Here's what I think I know and what I need next to better understand these terms and concepts:

This is a flexible target that will work with most topics

Force and Motion Vocabulary Builder Think Sheet

Learning Target: As I read, observe, and experiment I can build new vocabulary by synthesizing what I know and wonder about terms and concepts.

Word Bank Possibilities: force, motion, mass, friction, kinetic energy, height, speed, acceleration, inertia, Newton's Laws of Motion, gravity, balance

Students → *can choose their words or the teacher can select ones to meet students' needs.*

Vocabulary	What I Know	Diagram/Example	What I Wonder
Force	A force is a push or pull.	Force squishes an object	What kind of forces are there? I know that gravity or gravitational force is one.
Motion	This seems too easy. I know it is movement but how does it connect to these other terms?		
Inertia			I think this has to do movement of an object and friction but I'm not sure how.
Friction	I think it has something to do with slowing or changing the object's direction.	I'm thinking about swimming and how the water might change my motion when I dive. Maybe it has something to do with the push and pull of two object.	I think inertia is connected in some way to friction but I'm not sure how. Is friction another force?
Newton's First Law of Motion	I have no clue what this is. *Modeling confusion*		

Introducing to students that there are different kinds of forces

Modeling a need to know more.

Here's what I think I know and need next to better understand these terms and concepts:
I need to read more to figure out how all these terms connect. I know that the more I understand how they work together, I will be able to articulate what Newton's Laws of Motion are.

In my response, I model how I am setting a purpose for the next class. My response also emphasizes the need to connect individual terms to a bigger concept like Newton's Laws of Motion.

Connect Two

Learning Target: I can explain how terms are connected to each other and the topic I am studying.

I would connect _____ to _____ because _____

_____

I would connect _____ to _____ because _____

_____

I would connect _____ to _____ because _____

_____

I would connect _____ to _____ because _____

_____

Silent Reading Response Sheet

Date:

Learning Targets:

1.   I can increase my reading endurance to finish a book(s).

2.   I can monitor my inner voice to share what I remember reading.

3.   I can share what I've read to reflect new thinking.

Name:

Title of Book _____

Page on which I started _____ Page on which I ended _____ Total pages read _____

The time I started _____ The time I stopped _____ Total minutes read _____

How well did you meet the second learning target? What made you stop reading? What do you remember reading?

How well did you meet the third learning target? What were you thinking as you read? Try to write **FOUR** sentences. You might try to ask questions, make connections, give opinions, share new thoughts and/or ideas that you think are important.

Virtual Background Knowledge Placemats

To make this activity work virtually, you'll need some sort of virtual configuration, like chat rooms, to break students into small discussion groups.

Each student will need a thinksheet, similar to the one on the next page, to hold their connections, questions, and surprises. Section off the thinksheet to accommodate room for a title or description of the background knowledge placemat that you want students to read and respond to. In a virtual setting, I would provide no more than four choices.

As a whole group, show the first background knowledge placemat to the class. Give students time to study the images and then time to record connections, questions, and surprises. Once students have viewed the different background knowledge placemats, put them into virtual small groups so they can share their thinking. Visit each small group to listen for connections, questions, and surprising thinking that you want to highlight for the large group.

Pull students back together as a class. Being mindful of time, share the powerful thinking that you heard in each virtual small group. Offer students an opportunity to go back to their thinksheet to add new thoughts they had as a result of hearing your synthesis. Ask students to submit their thinksheets so you can create a whole-class document capturing examples of students' thinking. Share the class document with students at the next whole-class meeting.

(In lieu of sticky notes, use this thinksheet on the next page to capture student thinking.)

Virtual Background Knowledge Placemat Thinksheet
Student Example

Weapons of War Placemat	Picture of Omran Daqneesh and Letter from Alex
Connections:	**Connections:** This reminds me of the Holocaust. The Germans were killing their own people like the president of Syria.
Questions: Why is the Syrian president bombing his own people?	**Questions:** How did President Obama get Alex's letter? Did he ever respond to Alex?
Surprises: I'm surprised that barrel bombs are so cheap to make.	**Surprises:**
(Description of Placemat)	**(Description of Placemat)**

References

Alabed, Bana. 2018. *Dear World: A Syrian Girl's Story of War and Plea for Peace*. New York: Simon and Schuster.

Annas, George J., and Michael A. Grodin. 1995. *The Nazi Doctors and the Nuremburg Code*. New York: Oxford University Press.

Bennett, Samantha. 2007. *That Workshop Book: New Systems and Structures for Classrooms That Read, Write, and Think*. Portsmouth, NH: Heinemann.

Berger, Ron, Libby Woodfin, Suzanne Nathan-Plaut, Cheryl Dobbertin, Anne Vilen, and Leah Rugen. 2014. *Transformational Literacy: Making the Common Core Shift with Work that Matters*. San Francisco, CA: Jossey-Bass.

Brown, Peter C., Henry L. Roediger, and Mark A. McDaniel. 2014. *Make It Stick: The Science of Successful Learning*. Cambridge, MA: Harvard University Press.

Bruner, Jerome. 1962. *The Process of Education*. Cambridge, MA: Harvard University Press.

Bush, Laura. 2018. "Separating Children from Their Parents at the Border Breaks My Heart." *Washington Post*, June 17.

Common Core State Standards Initiative. www.corestandards.org.

deMarrais, Kathleen Bennett, and Margaret D. LeCompte. 1999. *The Way Schools Work: A Sociological Analysis of Education*. New York: Longman.

Emerson, Ralph Waldo. 1841, 1993. *Self-Reliance and Other Essays*. Mineola, NY: Dover Thrift Editions.

Fredricks, J. A., P. C. Blumenthfeld, and A. H. Paris. 2004. "School Engagement: Potential of the Concept, State of Evidence." *Review of Educational Research* 74 (1): 59–109.

Gratz, Alan. 2017. *Refugee*. New York: Scholastic.

Graves, Donald. 2002. *Testing Is Not Teaching: What Should Count in Education*. Portsmouth, NH: Heinemann.

Guthrie, John T. 2002. "Preparing Students for High-Stakes Test Taking in Reading." In *What Research Has to Say About Reading Instruction*, ed. Alan Farstrup and S. Jay Samuels. Newark, DE: International Reading Association.

Guthrie, John T. 2004. *Motivating Reading Comprehension: Concept-Orientated Reading Instruction*, ed. Allan Wigfield and Kathleen Perencevich. Mahwah, NJ: Lawrence Erlbaum Associates.

Hattie, John, and Gregory Yates. 2014. *Visible Learning and the Science of How We Learn*. New York: Routledge.

Hosseini, Khaled. 2003. *The Kite Runner*. New York: Riverhead Books.

Hunt, Jilly. 2018. *Human Rights for All*. Chicago: Heinemann Raintree.

Innocenti, Roberto, and Cristophe Gallaz. 1985. *Rose Blanche*. Mankato, MN: Creative Paperbacks.

Inslee, Jay. 2015. "Why My State Won't Close Its Doors to Syrian Refugees." *New York Times*, November 20.

The Jason Project. n.d. "Coaster Creator." October, 2018. https://assets.jason.org/resource_assets/4851/8673/coaster.html.

Keene, Ellin, and Susan Zimmerman. 1997. *Mosaic of Thought: Teaching Comprehension in a Reader's Workshop*. Portsmouth, NH: Heinemann.

Kopilow, Rachel. 2016. "A Six-Year-Old's Letter to the President: 'We Will Give Him a Family.'" *The White House: President Barack Obama* (blog), September, 21, 2016. https://obamawhitehouse.archives.gov/blog/2016/09/21/six-year-olds-letter-president-we-will-give-him-family.

Kullab, Samya, and Jackie Roche. 2017. *Escape from Syria*. Richmond Hill, ON Canada: Firefly Books.

McCarney, Rosemary. 2017. *Where Will I Live?* Toronto, ON Canada: Second Story Press.

Melville, Herman. *Moby Dick*. 1851. New York: Harper.

Mochizuki, Ken. 2009. *Baseball Saved Us*. New York: Harcourt School.

Orwell, George. 2003. *1984*. New York: Plume.

Puglise, Nicole. 2016. "Obama Cites Letter from Child Offering Home to Young Syrian Refugee." *The Guardian*, September 22. https://www.theguardian.com/us-news/2016/sep/22/obama-letter-alex-syrian-refugee-child.

Sanchez, Raf. 2017. "New Photos Emerge of Omran Daqneesh, the Boy Who Became a Symbol of Aleppo's Suffering," *The Telegraph*, June 5. https://www.telegraph.co.uk/news/2017/06/05/new-photos-emerge-omran-daqneesh-boy-became-symbol-aleppos-suffering/.

Senzai, N. H. 2018. *Escape from Aleppo*. New York: Simon and Schuster Books for Young Readers.

Steinbeck, John. 2002. *Of Mice and Men*. Steinbeck centennial ed. New York: Penguin.

Tovani, Cris, and Elizabeth Birr Moje. 2017. *No More Telling as Teaching: Less Lecture, More Engaged Learning*. Portsmouth, NH: Heinemann.

Tovani, Cris. 2000. *I Read It, but I Don't Get It: Comprehension Strategies for Adolescent Readers*. Portsmouth, NH: Stenhouse.

Tovani, Cris. 2004. *Do I Really Have to Teach Reading? Content Comprehension, Grades 6–12*. Portsmouth, NH: Stenhouse.

Tovani, Cris. 2011. *So What Do They Really Know? Assessment That Informs Teaching and Learning*. Portsmouth, NH: Stenhouse.

USA Today. 2018. "Your Say." June 19.

Wiesel, Elie. 1982. *Night*. Reissue ed. New York: Bantam Books.

Wolk, Steven. 2002. *Being Good: Rethinking Classroom Management and Student Discipline*. Portsmouth, NH: Heinemann.

Index